CLASSIC BLENDED SCOTCH

In the same series:

CLASSIC BLENDED SCOTCH

JIM MURRAY

To Max and Stephen Griggs for their help,
kindness and friendship.
Many heartfelt thanks.

First published in 1999 in Great Britain by
Prion Books Limited
Imperial Works
Perren Street
London NW5 3ED

© PRION BOOKS LIMITED 1999
Text copyright © Jim Murray 1999
Designed by DW Design

All rights reserved.

No part of this book may be reproduced,
stored in a retrieval system, or transmitted in any form
or by any means, electronic, mechanical,
photocopying, recording or otherwise, without the
prior written permission of the publisher.

A CIP record for this book is available from the
British Library

ISBN 1-85375-297-5

Cover design: Bob Eames
Printed and bound in China

PICTURE CREDITS
Illustrated London News 68-9
Mary Evans Picture Library 171
Public Record Office 6, 10, 22, 58
Still Moving Picture Library 122, 147, 196, 204
United Distillers 26
Vintage Magazine Archive 13, 71, 135, 143, 246

CONTENTS

PREFACE

It doesn't seem that long ago I was campaigning to get people to take an interest in single malt whisky. It was a hard sub-species to find. The world, it seemed, was dominated by blended Scotch. Some 15 years on and the circle has been completed. Now I'm desperately trying to get people to give blends a chance. Single malts have taken on a life of their own, which is no bad thing. But the situation is much today as it was fifteen years ago: I would ask features editors if they would like an article on whisky and I was treated as if my next stop should be a room with a padded cell. Malts beyond Glenfiddich and Glenmorangie were hardly known and that meant I obviously wanted to write something about Bells, or Haig or Teachers or, to them, something equally as squalid. The general rule was that the only drinks noble enough for column inches were wine or brandy. Likewise, if I ask an editor today if they would like an article on a blend, usually the answer is no, but something on malts might be quite acceptable.

Perhaps that goes to explain why, quite extraordinarily, this is the first ever book in the world dedicated exclusively to blended whisky, giving not only histories but, vitally, full tasting

Opposite
The once-high profile of blended Scotch whisky has in recent years been dominated by single malts. However, in 1905 at the time of this poster, single malt whisky was regarded as "too strong" for common consumption.

notes. It is a book that has given blends the malt treatment. I know the Scotch industry feels that such a book is long overdue; I'm hoping that, once you have been tempted to try some of the blends included in this book, you will too.

For my money there are just too many single malts on the market that are, well, boring. They have little to say for themselves and have to depend on evocative packaging to create an image. However, inside blended whiskies these same dull malts take on an extraordinary versatility: perhaps adding just a hint of something here, combining with another small group of otherwise unexceptional malts to create an aroma or flavour there which can simply beguile. It is no coincidence that the vast majority of Scotland's blenders – who are also responsible for the single malts on the shelves – usually prefer a blend when they choose their dram. And truth to tell, so do I.

I know no blend can, for me, match an Ardbeg in all its all-consuming, subtle magnificence or perhaps a Talisker for its firepower, a Springbank for its unfettered brilliance or an exceptional cask of Glenturret for its élan. There are, of course, some quite appalling blends, especially at the economy end of the market. But just how many malts can reach the heights of the truly extraordinary, labyrinthine Johnnie Walker Black, the delicacy of a Baillie Nicol Jarvie or a Lawson's 12, the multi-layered density of a

Teacher's or White Horse, the sheen of a Blue Hanger, the flawed genius of a Grant's or Original Mackinlay?

With the plethora of recent books on whisky (some good, the majority, sadly, rather poor) and the God-like status they normally bestow on malts, it is easy to conclude that they are the pinnacle of Scotch whisky. The truth, as you will discover over the following pages, is something quite different and something blenders have known but kept quiet about for a very long time: rather than progress on to malts, it is the blend which represents the ultimate challenge for whisky connoisseur and lover alike.

Jim Murray
Wellingborough 1999

"Friar Royd"

FINE OLD SCOTCH WHISKY

JAMES H. S. HOLROYD,

19, ST DUNSTAN'S HILL, LONDON, E.C. AND AT GLASGOW.

CHAPTER ONE

THE ERA OF ENLIGHTENMENT

A HISTORY OF BLENDED SCOTCH

It may seem hard to believe, perhaps because it gives the impression of having been around for ever, but blended Scotch is the new kid on the block, the baby of the whisky family. It is predated by single malt, single grain, Irish, Canadian, bourbon and rye. And although Tennessee whiskey has been officially designated as such since only 1941, it is almost certain that the filtration method which sets that particular whisky apart was around before a gentleman called Andrew Usher and some like-minded businessmen began mixing single malt Scotch and single grain Scotch to produce one of the tastiest hybrids of all time.

That was in a year adjacent to 1860 when a change in the law was to alter the shape of whisky production for ever. Until that time a succession of complex duty laws meant that it had not been possible to blend malt and grain whiskies together. At first the Act of 1860 had hit the distiller hard: duty had been raised, seemingly through the roof, and the immediate

Opposite
Praise be to blended Scotch, the saviour of Scotland's malt distilleries.

result was a fall in whisky demand. But slowly the penny dropped: the door had been left ajar for a whole new dimension to be added to a still embryonic industry. It was the door that was to eventually lead to the development of the most popular spirit in the world.

The evolution of Scotch from a base, simple spirit distilled illicitly in the remotest glens of the Scottish Highlands to a sophisticated one, that no self-respecting gentleman would find his home without, was long and complicated. As in most cases of evolution, there was to be more than one species living side by side, with the weaker dying out as the stronger ones not only survived but thrived.

No-one really knows when it all began. In Ireland there are fanciful tales of 13th-century English invaders discovering whiskey being made there, although not a scrap of hard evidence. Certainly by 1494 whisky was being made in Scotland. The Exchequer Rolls for that year clearly state: "*Eight bolls of malt to Friar John Cor, by order of the King, to make aqua vitae.*" Three years later an item in the Accounts of the Lord High Treasurer of Scotland listed: "*To the barbour that brocht aqua vitae to the King in Dundee, by the King's Command, 9s.*" The latter entry is fascinating but the first is irrefutable: it clearly states malt as the staple for the *aqua vitae*, the water of life. And not only that, but single malt whisky to boot. All previous mentions of

The Same Safe Old Stimulant

"My stand-by for over 50 Years — Dewar's"

Left
Blended Scotch was often portrayed as a sign of rude health and high status.

aqua vitae either referred to wine or, as in the Dundee entry, no specific ingredient at all. For that reason the Scotch whisky industry marked 1994 as the celebration of its 500th birthday.

For the first 333 of those years malt, or at least barley, was the vital, indeed sole, seed for Scotch whisky and the pot its womb. Most of it was made illegally, especially by farmers in the winter months looking to make maximum capital out of their barley, and drunk locally or perhaps finding its way from the Highlands into the larger cities and towns of the Lowlands thanks to the industry which ran parallel to distillation: smuggling. By the 17th century some whisky had made its way into England, although it hardly registered against the mainstays of gin for the lower classes and brandy for the higher. Beer was also popular throughout Britain (as it had to be when water was so often the bearer of disease and death, especially in urban areas) and as its quality improved so did its popularity. Maybe it was this appreciation of malt liquor from cradle to grave that helped acclimatise people's tastes towards whisky as a preferred spirit. In any case, it was a time when the drinking of alcohol was a basic necessity to sustain life.

The way the whisky had been made for those centuries in Scotland was very much like the method employed by Friar John Cor. He would have used the malted barley to make a beer and then distilled the alcohol from the liquid with the use of a pot, almost certainly fashioned from copper. It was a relatively simple operation and effective. However, for distillers who saw the making of whisky as a genuinely commercial, legal enterprise the use of a pot still was an expensive tradition. What they required was apparatus that could distil much more efficiently: continuously rather than in the stop-start batch method dictated by pots.

It has often – and wrongly – been claimed that

the search for a still that would work continuously was confined to the British Isles. Certainly it was the ingenuity of two men in particular, Robert Stein and Aeneas Coffey, that changed the way in which whisky would be made, with those two men playing a role essential to the development of Scotch whisky. But it should not be overlooked that elsewhere enormous energy was being expended on finding a way of making whisky cheaply, especially in North America where the industries of Pennsylvania, Kentucky and Canada were burgeoning at a rate even faster than in Scotland. And in America, a full ten years before Stein made his breakthrough, distillers had devised methods of producing whiskey by a form of patent distillation much more efficient than the traditional pot method.

Stein, himself a distiller, was the first to successfully harness a method in which live steam could be used to have direct contact with the malted barley beer, to wash and strip the alcohols for condensation. In 1827 he registered his ground-breaking patent, numbered 5583, and a year later followed up with a modified version numbered 5721. He had certainly hit upon the most efficient method by theory, but in practice his stills had a tendency to be hard to control. It was not until 1830 that distillers were finally offered a still that worked with remarkable reliability: the Coffey still. So dependable has

Above
*The famous
19th-century
scene of the Still
House at
Bowmore
distillery, Islay.
Here the two
larger copper pots
are the wash
stills; the spirit
stills are the
thinner ones. In
those days stills
were coal fired.*

that invention been that they are still in use today. The originals were made of wood, usually pine, although today they are made from metal and can be found at grain distilleries such as Port Dundas and North British. It is curious, though, that Coffey's patent made no mention of the word "whisky": it refers only to "wash" and "alcohol". That, plus the fact that Stein was one of five distillers who made spirit predominantly for the English market, has led to a now century-year-old argument that the first continuous stills in Britain (as opposed to the US) were never designed with whisky in mind at all, but for the making of a high proof spirit to be used for further rectification for gin or non-beverage use. That may be so, but even if true

16

there is still no doubting the impact they were to make on the future development of Scotch whisky.

Back in the 1830s British distillers were still tied to using barley for continuous distillation by the Corn Laws, although they did make big savings in both manpower and the amount of coal required. It was not until the repeal of the Corn Laws in 1846, when distillers were given the chance to buy cheaper, imported grain, notably maize, that the Coffey still began making a spirit which would become recognisable to future generations of whisky blenders. However, there is no firm evidence that they did so until the 1860s. The Coffey stills were swiftly implemented at the Cameronbridge distillery, even though it was owned by the famous Haig family who were themselves related to Stein. For many years Stein and Coffey stills worked side by side. The Coffey still was adapted to work from maize to produce grain spirit while the Stein stills distilled from malted barley to make what was known as "silent malt".

It was only a considerable time after the 1860 legislation which had allowed whisky merchants to mix these different codes of whisky together under bond that any attempt was made to define exactly what whisky was. This was not a question that taxed the first blenders. Men like Andrew Usher had already been working with whisky, attempting to find fresh markets, and were aware

that the further spirit travelled south the harder
it became to find stable markets. Arthur Bell of
Perth, John Walker of Kilmarnock, William
Teacher of Glasgow and many others had all
started off as local grocers in which capacity they
also supplied wines and spirits to a parochial
trade. The first whiskies they would have sold
would have been pure malts, mainly Highland
and usually direct from the cask. Only as they
and their heirs tried to develop their business
nationally and internationally did they discover

that people preferred something lighter than malt whisky, even that which had been a mixture of Highlands and Lowlands. Customers in England and throughout the Empire found the flavour of Highland whisky much peatier and oilier than is the case today, simply too dynamic. For that reason Irish whiskey, and that from Dublin in particular, was for many years much more appreciated than Scotch outside Scotland; probably for being in the main lighter on account of it having been usually triple distilled, made without the use of the turf and, perhaps most importantly of all, being a mixture of malted and unmalted barley. Proof of this can be seen in the sales of whisky by W. & A. Gilbey. By 1875 a fraction over two out every three bottles they sold was Irish. One of the reasons for this phenomenon was that until 1905 Gilbey, owners of Strathmill and Glen Spey distilleries, refused to sell anything other than whisky in its purest form. For them, blends were not an option until the turn of the century when they gave way to "public demand". However, Irish distilleries (those in Belfast apart) pointedly refused to take the blended path and fought a rearguard action against the ubiquitous grain spirit by insisting that their product be untainted by it. It proved to be their downfall.

In Scotland independent malt whisky distillers fought hard to prevent grain distillers calling their produce "whisky". They had been given the

Opposite
Once, all distilleries cut peat for their own maltings. Today only a handful of distilleries continue malting and as a consequence malt whiskies tend to be less peaty than a generation ago.

chance to fight their corner by Islington Council in north London, whose officials were clearly irked at the quality of spirits on sale in their local hostelries. In 1904 they took successful action against those selling a brandy they deemed unfit for the name, with neutral spirit included in the drink. A year later they took two more merchants to court, one for selling Irish and the other Scotch. Both samples were found to contain just 10 per cent of spirit that had been pot distilled and neither whisky was more than a year old. Again they won their case. The action of Islington Council caused national interest and massive concern throughout the Scotch whisky industry. By this time there were hundreds of blending companies producing a vast array of brands. The biggest owned both grain and malt distillers, the largest being the Distillers Company Limited. But this was also the age of the Whisky Baron, when larger-than-life characters toured the world selling their company's whisky and making Scotch whisky a bastion of respectability. Most notable among them were Tommy Dewar and Jimmy Buchanan, and while they were not responsible for selling whisky of tender age and of such dubious quality, the use of grain whisky in their brands and the right to call it Scotch was paramount to their continued success.

The industry was still recovering from one catastrophe: the failure of Pattison's. This

Opposite
Jimmy Buchanan toured the world making Scotch whisky a bastion of respectability and became an aristocrat into the bargain.

Right
*Whisky
companies tried
to impress the
public with the
alleged purity of
their product at
a time when the
quality of a
dram was often
open to debate.
Here some light
humour has been
added for good
measure.*

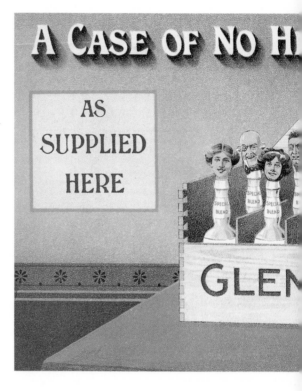

company had risen steeply from obscurity and vanished again, leaving shock waves pounding through the whisky world. The Pattison brothers had traded fraudulently, overvaluing their stocks and obtaining vast credit to keep afloat a lavish lifestyle, a massive team of salesmen and an advertising campaign that made their name known the length and breadth of the Empire. At the time of the company's demise in 1898 banks

had already begun fearing that excessive amounts of their money had been sunk into projects that were exacerbating the problem. Too much whisky was being made and not enough was being drunk. When Pattison's crashed and the brothers were subsequently jailed, banks needed no second urging to withdraw. Many companies failed or were swallowed up by larger ones. For companies like DCL who were powerful enough to withstand the crisis this was a good opportunity to pick up stocks and brands at rock bottom prices.

The "What is Whisky?" case was another matter entirely. A Royal Commission was set up to decide on the matter and if they found against grain spirit then each and every blending house could be facing severe difficulties. As part of the propaganda battle that ensued, DCL launched a pure grain whisky onto the market, a 7-year-old Cambus, taking a full page advertisement in the *Daily Mail* to do so. It made a point of saying it was not a pot still whisky and defined its purity as not affecting the liver nor having a headache in a gallon's-worth – neither claim of which was remotely true. This was as much light-heartedly cocking a snook at the malt distillers as seriously bringing to public attention the quality of grain whisky: Cambus was always regarded the finest of the continuous whiskies. On their part some malt distillers were willing perhaps to go so far as accepting anything bearing the name Scotch whisky that might contain up to 50 per cent grain but no more; others preferred to see grain outlawed altogether. As it happened, in 1909 the Royal Commission decided in favour of the grain distillers but not before holding thirty-seven sittings and questioning 116 witnesses into just about every facet concerning the making and marketing of whisky and the physical consequences of its consumption. They did not decide on what age or strength whisky should be as that was beyond their jurisdiction; that legislation came during World War I. (In 1915 the Immature Spirits Act stipulated that all whisky must be matured for two years; in 1916 it was raised to three; in 1917 it was declared that whisky had to be a minimum 70 proof – 40 per cent ABV.)

The grain distillers had won, and so too had the Scotch whisky industry. For what is beyond doubt is that had the Commission found the case for the malt distillers, Scotch whisky would never have been as popular as it became throughout the 20th century. Today 94 out of every 100 bottles of Scotch whisky is a blend, usually containing around 25–35 per cent malt whisky. Had the public turned its back on the heavy flavour of pure malt, it is hard to imagine more than a small fraction of Scotland's nearly one hundred distilleries still being around today. When the great entrepreneurial families of the 19th century are listed – the Haigs, Teachers, Dewars, Walkers, Grants, Mackies, Buchanans, Bells, Ballantines and dozens more – it is worth remembering that they set sail with fair economic winds to their backs but into the unknown and guided only by their brave hearts and an unquenchable belief in a new type of whisky that uniquely revealed and celebrated the combined beauty of the fruits of Scotland's distilleries. Large and small.

CHAPTER TWO

GOING WITH THE GRAIN

HOW SCOTCH WHISKY IS MADE

A vital element of enjoying a good blend is to understand just what roles the constituent parts play. A blended Scotch is, after all, a marriage of two quite different characters and cultures. And like most marriages some work and others don't. The main task of the blender is to ensure blissful harmony. And for the drinker the fun is heightened by an appreciation of how those almost polarised grain spirits somehow unite to form a character all their own.

Most whisky drinkers understand that blended whisky is different to malt whisky, although few can tell you exactly what that difference is. It is reasonably common knowledge that the blend will contain whisky from more than one distillery while a single malt is just that: a whisky from one distillery. But to be a blend, a whisky must contain something other than malt whisky, and that is grain whisky. It makes sense, therefore, before going any further into the book to understand the fundamental and quite simple

Opposite
Barley plays a vital part in the blend of a Scotch whisky.

Below
*Traditional floor
maltings, where
the soaked grain
is left to
germinate,
remain the most
atmospheric
section of the few
distilleries still
using them.*

difference between malt and grain whisky.

Malt whisky, as we have seen, is how it all began. It was the first whisky, made from barley. Grain whisky on the other hand will also contain barley, but about 90 per cent will be made from wheat or maize. And they are made in a quite different way, as we shall see.

MALT WHISKY

In this case, barley is steeped in water for between 48 and 60 hours until it doubles in weight. It is then either spread on the ground on

what is called a floor maltings or put into metallic containers where the grain is mechanically turned. Over the forthcoming days the waterlogged grain begins to develop shoots. This shows that the chemical composition of the grain has turned from being starch-rich to sugar-rich. It is this sugar, an energy source for the shoots within the grain, that will be used to make whisky. To keep as much sugar as possible in the grain it is then quickly dried over a kiln. The amount of smokiness the whisky shall eventually display will depend mainly on the amount of peaty smoke that is absorbed by the barley during kiln drying. On Islay, for instance, vast quantities of peat are used in kilning; elsewhere very little.

When the now malted barley has dried it is then milled: that means it is crushed or hammered into a powder called the grist. The grist is then added to hot water that dissolves and strains the sugars from the grist. This is called mashing. The grist is mashed three times, with the waters from the weaker third mash being used as the first water to dissolve the sugars from the next mash. This sugar-rich solution is called wort.

The wort is then pumped in wash backs for fermentation. Here yeast is added, which feeds upon the sugars to produce in equal measure carbon dioxide and, vitally, alcohol. As the yeast acts upon the wort the solution turns from sweet to bitter as the sugars are consumed. The more bitter it becomes, the more alcohol the liquid, now called wash, contains. Finally, after anything between 40 and 78 hours the frothing has stopped and a muddy-coloured beer of about 8 per cent alcohol by volume is left.

Now distillation can take place. The wash is entered into a copper pot still, usually onion-

Left
Copper pot stills turn a barley 'beer' called wash into a clear spirit which, after three years in oak casks, can be called whisky.

shaped, which acts as a giant kettle. The first still is called the wash still. When the still is heated the first vapours to be given off contain alcohol since that evaporates faster than water. These vapours rise and pass through the head of the still and continue into a tubular copper device called a condenser, or into a more traditional copper coil called a worm which is submerged in cold water in a vessel know as a worm tub. These low wines, a spirit containing about 20 per cent alcohol, are then passed into a second still, the spirit still. The low wines are reheated in the second still. The very first vapours contain unwanted elements that are separated and redistilled. It is only when the stillman sees that the distillation has reached the heart of the run that he turns the swivel spout in the spirit safe towards the receiver. Towards the end of the run the spirit becomes too weak and these tails, like the heads, have to be redistilled. (In very rare cases in Scotland triple distillation takes place and the second still is called the intermediate still.)

The spirit selected for barrelling, or filling as it is termed, is then reduced with water, usually from the same source used for mashing. It is taken down from around 71 per cent ABV to 63.5 per cent ABV. Then the spirit is entered into an oak barrel and matured in warehouses. Only when this spirit reaches its third birthday in the cask does it then legally become Scotch whisky.

GRAIN WHISKY

The route to producing mash for distillation is just about the same as in the making of malt whisky except, because the principal ingredient of grain whisky is unmalted wheat or maize, cookers have to be used to break down the hardy walls containing the starchy innards. Maize does not easily lend itself to malting so once it is cooked it is then added to either green malt, that is the germinated barley before it has been kiln dried, or peat-free kiln-dried malt. Enzymes from the malt convert the starches released during the cooking of the maize into sugars. It is these sugars which trigger off the feeding frenzy in the yeast which has been added for fermentation. Likewise, unmalted wheat is cooked and the resultant slurry added to malt and the process is repeated. In each case about 10 per cent of the mash is malt, although one grain distiller prefers to use up to 25 per cent for flavouring reasons.

Instead of this maize or wheat wash being entered into a pot still, continuous stills are used. There are usually two: an analyser and rectifier. In simple terms the wash is poured into the top of a column and, as it falls, live steam is pumped from the bottom upwards. The fall of the wash is slowed by a number of perforated plates, usually of copper, sometimes of stainless steel, which allows the fluid to fall downwards and the steam to carry in the

opposite direction. When the two meet, the steam strips the alcohol from the wash and carries it at anything between 10 per cent ABV and 20 per cent ABV to a second, rectifying, still where the same principle is used. This still takes the vapour to a higher strength of around 94 per cent ABV before it is at last allowed to condense as grain spirit.

Above
Green malt helps convert the starches released during the cooking of grains into sugars.

33

FIRST IN QUALITY... FIRST IN FLAVOR

1627 First Still...

1948 Still First

In unvarying high quality and mellow flavor Haig & Haig
Scotch Whisky reflects the world-wide reputation of
Scotland's oldest distillers. Today the demand for
this famous Scotch Whisky is greater than ever before.

Don't be Vague... say **Haig & Haig**

BLENDED SCOTS WHISKY, 86.8 PROOF • RENFIELD IMPORTERS LTD, NEW YORK

CHAPTER THREE

GRAIN WHISKY DISTILLERIES

CAMERONBRIDGE

This is the grand-daddy continuous distillery of them all, its history inseparable from that of the famous Haig whisky name and the development of Scotch whisky. The bridge in Fife from which one John Haig in 1822 viewed the Cameron Mill on the banks of the Leven still stands today. Distilling had already been in his family's blood for generations, and now he had left university the young Haig surveyed the site, already sensing that this was where his fame and fortune would lie. Backed by his father he secured the tenancy for the land and began building his distillery. But this was not to be just another Scottish distillery: he was related to Alexander Stein and it was he who was pioneering work with continuous distillation. He built the distillery around Stein's new-fangled stills, but soon discovered that another patent type, one made by Aeneas Coffey, produced a better spirit more efficiently. In business money is thicker than blood and the Coffey stills became synonymous with Cameronbridge's whisky, and even today there

Opposite
The name Haig has become indelibly linked with the Cameronbridge grain distillery.

are three relatively state-of-the-art Coffeys in operation. There was still a place for Stein's cumbersome apparatus at Cameronbridge, as well as a traditional pot still, right up until the time Alfred Barnard visited in the 1880s, when he reported an astounding abundance of whisky styles being made there, including patent "Grain Whisky", "Pot Still Irish", "Silent Malt" and "Flavoured Malt". Very little of the original plant and buildings survive to this day, the stillhouse now being of the glass variety. But the wheated grain made there is top quality stuff used in every traditional blend produced by owners United Distillers and Vintners, including the Johnnie Walker family of blends and, of course, Haig. The major character is a very gentle sweet softness that tends to form a dais for the better malts to preach from. Despite a single grain called Cameron Brig being a firm favourite around nearby Windygates and elsewhere in Fife, to see this grain to best effect it is worth tracking down a bottle of 12-year-old, a cream-toffee dram about as silky a whisky as you are likely to find.

DUMBARTON

Defiantly facing the craggy island of Dumbarton Rock, as if refusing to be intimidated by its 250-foot twin peaks, this distillery is perhaps the most imposing sight in the whole Scotch whisky industry. The sum total of over two million red bricks, it is almost a mirror reflection of its sister

distillery 3000 miles away at Walkerville, Ontario, home of Canadian Club. Dumbarton's history is told under the Ballantine section, as it was built by Hiram Walker-Gooderham and Worts to supply the grain for their recently acquired Ballantine brand. The distillery, although a 1930s creation, remains one of the most charming of all Scotland's grain plants.

Above

The massive red-brick Dumbarton distillery remains an imposing quay-side sight.

Much of its original design and workings are still going strong although the enormous warehousing facilities and malt distillery built at the time, Inverleven, are now redundant. The distillery, now owned by Allied Domecq, has stuck to its guns by continuing to distil from maize, although it is geared to use wheat as well. The maize is easily the more complex whisky of the two: the wheat is not as sweet as some others made from that particular grain but lacks the rigidity and firm direction of the Indian corn.

GIRVAN

This is another distillery which looks out onto a famous rock off the Scottish coast, although Ailsa Craig is much further away from Girvan than Dumbarton is to its own little island. Until the day Bladnoch hopefully returns to production, this remains the southernmost working distillery in Scotland. It is found on the outskirts of Girvan, Ayrshire, and was built in 1963 by William Grant, with the redundant construction workers asked to complete the job inside the plant by turning their hand to making the whisky. The stills, in a North American style, are located outside the buildings and, enduring the full blast of winter winds off the sea, have been known to freeze over. The distillery converted from maize to wheat in 1985 and some blenders believe this is one of the few that benefited by doing so: Girvan's is perhaps the most improved grain whisky over the last decade, showing an appreciated firmness not always found in wheat grain spirit. It can be bought as a single grain through their deliciously impressive and vaguely bourbony export and duty-free brand Black Barrel.

INVERGORDON

The only grain distillery operating in the Highlands, it is found nestling among homes in the Cromarty Firth port by that name. It was built as a grain plant in 1959, although between 1965 and 1977 it was also home to the Ben Wyvis malt distillery. This large grain distillery was the golden nugget that drew Whyte & Mackay into a protracted and eventually successful takeover battle that saw them absorb Invergordon Distillers. The grain made there is about as sweet as it gets: often a blend that shows a pronounced caramel character contains too much colouring agent, or it could just be the Invergordon. Some blenders when using Invergordon prefer also to include a firmer, maize-based grain like North British to give extra, sharper backbone to what could otherwise prove to be a softer, sweeter blend than they might require.

LOCH LOMOND

This is Scotland's newest grain distillery which, after a faltering start, is now producing 10 million litres of grain alcohol each year. Seven

million of that is used for the blends of the owners Glen Catrine, mainly for the low-price High Commissioner. The grain plant was built in 1994 and is situated adjacent to the Loch Lomond malt distillery at Alexandria. Wheat is used in preference to maize and the samples I have tasted have been impressively sweet and fat. Originally High Commissioner used mainly Strathclyde; since the switch to its own grain in 1997 the blend has softened and sweetened considerably. As well as supplying their own blends, they are also filling for Seagram and Morrison Bowmore. Despite its late arrival on the whisky scene, the distillery has links with distilling dating right back to 1817. The company is owned by Sandy Bulloch, who paid for the building of the grain plant in cash so that no interest would accrue. He is a direct descendant of the Bulloch distilling family that merged with D. Lade & Co. to form the famous Bulloch Lade company in 1855.

NORTH BRITISH

This sprawling distillery in the shadow of the famous Tynecastle stadium of Edinburgh's leading soccer club, Heart of Midlothian, can be regarded the first ever to be built especially for blended whisky. Although it was predated by a number of grain plants, their intention was to make cheaply a whisky that could help supplement and lighten more expensive and richer-flavoured malt

Opposite
Casks of the sweet Invergordon grain being stacked and stored by paletisation as opposed to the ancient racking system. This is to save space and manpower, but there are many who feel that casks do not have the same ability to breathe as before.

Above

Andrew Usher,
who pioneered
the art of
blending malt
and grain
whiskies, was
also responsible,
among others,
for the founding
of the North
British distillery.

whisky. Fearing the power of the Distillers Company and bent on breaking the price-fixing that was going on between rival grain whisky producers, a group of prominent and not-so-prominent blenders united to form their own company and build their own grain whisky distillery. Leading the group was Andrew Usher, who had pioneered the art of blending malt and grain whisky. Built in 1885 the distillery has somehow retained its air of independence and tradition, although now it is owned by UDV and Ederington Group (proprietors of Robertson & Baxter). It is the only grain distillery with its own maltings, although these days a kiln is superfluous: it uses green malt (barley that has been soaked and germinated but not kiln dried). A staggering 25 per cent of the mash is green malt, the remainder maize. What is more, Coffey stills are used. The result is the sharpest, tangiest, most strongly flavoured grain whisky on the market that is deserving of a wider appreciation as a single whisky at about eight to ten years. Blenders refer to it simply and affectionately as "NB". Almost to a species, they love it once an early trademark sulphury-ness has been tamed by the wood and, likewise, with the loss of Cambus, it is my favourite grain of them all. Most of all it is used to give sturdiness to a blend; especially light, Speyside-rich ones where too much sweetness would swamp the delicacy of the malts.

PORT DUNDAS

More Coffey stills are found at this old Glasgow distillery which is unusually located atop a hill. Port Dundas is famous for being the distillery where Alfred Barnard began his epic journey around all Scotland's and Ireland's distilleries in the mid-1880s and some of the external features he saw then are still there today – although for how much longer I dread to think. Port Dundas is found beside the Forth–Clyde Canal and, like North British and Cameronbridge, uses green malt. However, unlike NB and in keeping with the old United Distillers adopted style, it uses wheat as opposed to maize. Like Cameronbridge, Port Dundas finds its way into virtually all the traditional UD brands such as Johnnie Walker, Buchanan's, White Horse and so on.

STRATHCLYDE

Located in the notorious Gorbals area of Glasgow for the last 70 years, the distillery, also used in the production of Beefeater Gin (indeed, it was built in 1927 principally as a gin

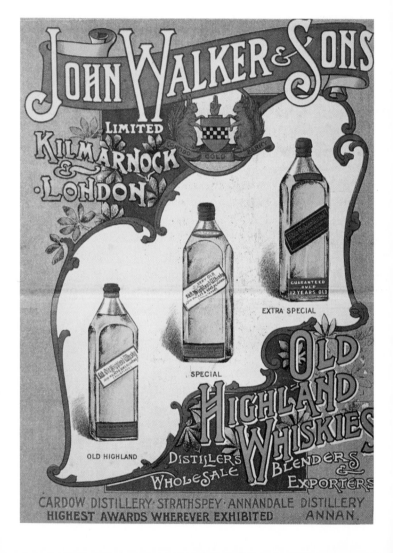

distillery), is crammed into a one-acre site beside the Clyde and makes a grain spirit that has to be treated with great care. Now owned by Allied Domecq, it was once part of the Long John empire, a fact evidenced by the stills being typically short on copper. It shows in the spirit, cabbage-watery at first, which blenders treat with very great respect if not necessarily affection. There are blenders who refuse outright to touch the stark wheat grain from that distillery until it is at least seven years old, sometimes older, preferring for it to have calmed down in the oak. Others will never allow more than 10 per cent of it in any one blend. But there are those who use it for its lively qualities at an older age in a bid to punch holes through any overpowering sweetness or blandness. Really something very different: a bucking bronco of a grain mastered, it must be said, by only the very bravest blenders.

Opposite

Like Cameronbridge, Port Dundas still finds its way into virtually all the traditional UD brands such as Johnnie Walker.

CHAPTER FOUR

A QUESTION OF BALANCE

LIFE INSIDE THE BLENDER'S LAB

This is the part of whisky making that is "off limits" to the hundreds of thousands of tourists and enthusiasts who flood into Scotland's distilleries each year. And for most it is probably just as well: a room with a sink, a number of cupboards filled with whisky samples of varying ages, some nosing glasses hanging bat-like from a specially designed rail, some measuring equipment and a person or two walking about the room, sniffing here, taking notes there. It is a long way removed from the clonking of newly filled casks being marched off to their warehouse, the frothing of the wash backs, the heat, hissing and rich malt-alcohol smell of the stillhouse.

For the advanced whisky connoisseur the blending lab is, however, every bit as fascinating as a distillery. For this is where the fruits of the combined knowledge of Scotland's stillmen, brewers and distillery managers are pulled together and a small, exclusive group of

Opposite
Rows of whiskies of varying ages, depths and fragrance, await the art of the whisky blender.

experienced men and women pit their highly developed sensory skills against the complex challenge of wood and spirit combined.

Blending whisky is not a straightforward matter of throwing a number of whiskies together. In every warehouse throughout Scotland there are any number of casks just waiting to trip up the blender, which is why quality control is so important. Part of the blender's job is to oversee quality control, which in relatively smaller companies can be done personally; or in larger ones people are specially employed to weed out any off-notes – although Richard Paterson at Whyte & Mackay makes a point of testing the barrels about to be used in a blend, dancing along the rows of casks, nosing spirit that has been added to warm water.

But first, vitally, before it ever comes to the act of blending, the spirit must be of a set standard coming off the still. And as it matures in oak it is possible for the spirit to somehow react adversely with the wood. Although it is rare it does happen and one bad cask can ruin an entire vatting if it gets through undetected. For that reason blenders of extremely light blends such as Cutty Sark, J&B and Famous Grouse have to be on constant vigil. If a sub-standard cask is rooted out, it may be quietly blended away in a full-bodied dram where it cannot be detected, just one or even half a barrel against many hundreds. That, curiously, is also why some blenders

Opposite
Casks of whisky are dumped into troughs, allowing a marrying process to begin before the blend is bottled.

49

actually select some of their better whiskies for their younger, cheaper, lighter blends.

Blending companies come in all shapes and sizes. And the stocks held by blenders will have a direct bearing on the type of blended whisky they will eventually produce. The largest of them all is United Distillers & Vintners who hold stocks approaching some 8 million casks of whisky. For that reason it is impossible for blender Maureen Robinson to sample every cask about to be used in one of the company's numerous blends. But every day she will be faced with a battery of nosing glasses, the front line being grains, the back being malts. They may be their own grains or malts or those brought in from other companies. The glasses contain clear spirit, revealing that it is "new make", fresh from the distillery. Whether the blends are destined to contain mainly 4- and 5-year-old whiskies or super de luxes boasting malts and grains of twenty years and more, it is imperative that a close track is kept on the whisky's development. So Maureen will run through the whiskies, summing them up with one word. For Oban, she will mark "clean" or "perfumed"; for Teaninich, "clean", "grassy" or sometimes "sweet" and "fruity"; for Clynelish, "waxy" or perhaps "vegetable" or "clean" or "grassy" or "sweet". Over the years, as many if not most distilleries almost imperceptibly change the style of their make (for instance, the fabulous Royal Lochnagar has moved away from spicy towards grassy), the language may alter accordingly; like most languages it has evolved over many years, in this case with successive blenders and assistants pitting their knowledge together. Other blenders also use their own terminology, although some prefer to work from the Whisky Wheel, a flavour guide developed by research scientists. It is curious, though, that the one used at UDV is almost identical to the one I have developed over the years for my own tasting purposes. Their compartments for malts are Clean, Fruity, Green/Grassy, Green/Oily, Meaty, Metallic, Musty, Nutty, Peaty, Perfumed, Sour, Spicy, Sulphury, Sweet, Vegetable, Waxy. Under Fruity you will find a sub-division of wine gums, pear drops, bubble gum, and so on. In my own laboratory, for instance, I have "smoky" (which is found under Peaty at UDV) as an entirely different category, with "spent fireworks" (cordite), "bonfires" and "pipe smoke" found as sub-species. For any laboratory, though, what is important is not so much the descriptive labels but the understanding between blenders of a type of aroma that the word refers to and just what that aroma means to any particular whisky. For instance, if a blender gets sulphury notes off new make North British grain, that is to be expected and will not cause any problems since the three years in the cask it takes for it to be designated Scotch will usually eradicate this note. However, if "sulphury" is marked against

Above

The blender's task is one of constant checking, nosing and tasting to ensure that a blend's individual style is maintained.

Port Dundas or Girvan, say, memos will fly.

This applies to all whiskies and all types of aroma. If Maureen's notes do not match the prescribed descriptors, alarm bells will sound and she will check the readings from a parallel tasting at the company's Elgin laboratories. If the result tallies, investigations will begin into why the spirit is not performing the way it is expected.

Similar tests are carried out throughout Scotland's laboratories. Curiously enough, most blenders – despite years of training – tend to know and understand only the whiskies that they deal with on a daily basis. No company, including the giant UDV, uses every whisky available. For that reason ask a blender of even 20 or 30 years' experience what they think about a certain malt (they usually understand all the grains) and they might admit that it has been over a dozen years since they last tasted it. And maybe never at all at over five years old.

However, it is the blenders' deep understanding of the malts they have to deal with, especially those owned by his company, that enables them to maintain standards even under testing circumstances. Sometimes a whisky that has been a mainstay of a blend for many years will no longer be available, either through a distillery being mothballed (closed down for a few years) or shut entirely. Then the blender will have to find a replacement. Because few whiskies are identical, often two or more whiskies will have to be used to substitute the single one lost. If the malt that has been lost is simply a "bulk" whisky of no great significance in character development of the brand but helps increase the malt content, usually it can be replaced without too much difficulty, as there are many "secondary" malts whose contribution to flavour is negligible. If, however, it is "top dressing" a leading malt of high character, the blender has to tread carefully.

Most blenders regard themselves as custodians of tried and trusted blends, their main purpose being to safeguard and perpetuate the style and quality of an established brand. While nearly all

Above

Some of the grains and malts that, together, become Johnnie Walker Red.

the blender's time is spent on the day-to-day routine of achieving this noble goal, there is nothing like the buzz of the lab when orders have come through for the development of a new blend, or even for an old one to be altered slightly. It is then that the creative juices of the blenders start running and being inside a lab during this time is perhaps my favourite part of the whisky-making cycle, distilleries included. Blenders will have been given a brief and now they must use their skills to match expectations. Some blends have been created in a day. Others

take up to a couple of weeks in the laboratory alone, and further time for it to get approved by the marketing people.

Before a blender puts a single whisky into a measuring jug, stock availability will first be checked. There is no point inventing a new blend if the whiskies used (and the types of casks they are carried in if a percentage of sherry butts are desired in the formula) will run out after a few months or years should marketing targets be met or exceeded, or if it will erode into stocks required for other blends or single malts. It is only when the blender is satisfied that he knows which materials he has to play with that the fun begins. Most blenders work to spirit reduced to 20 per cent alcohol by volume, half the strength at which it will usually be bottled. One or two do prefer working with slightly stronger spirit, although, remarkably, some blends make their way into bottles without the blenders tasting it at all, having used their nose alone. That practice, though, is becoming increasingly unusual – but not yet extinct as there is a blender I know who actually dislikes the taste of whisky!

If the customer is from outside the company

and looking for an "economy" (i.e. cheap) brand, then grain will play a vital role. Some blenders may use 75/80 grain to 25/20 malt, although those malts might be mainly secondaries. Not all malts are highly prized by blenders. Some are used simply to "bulk up" the malt content without using too much of the malts, which are treasured for their ability to have a direct influence on the flavour profile of the blend. Others may use up to 90 per cent grain but the 10 per cent malt used will be "top dressing", full of character and flavour, to make amends. The brief may be for a high quality blend. Then the grain-to-malt ratio is of little consequence. But no matter what kind of whisky they are producing they have to treat Islay malts with kid gloves: the powerful peaty character can quickly throw a blend off line and just 4 per cent of an Islay malt can have a significant say in whether the blend is regarded as light or heavy. On 4 per cent and above you are definitely hitting the weighty side, which some blenders will desire. What the blender will be looking for, above all, is balance. And that, if you ask any blender, is the secret, the golden key, to a fine blend.

A Summary of How Blended Whisky Is Made
1. Grain and malt whisky made in Scotland's distilleries.
2. Whiskies (and under-aged spirit) selected for a brand will be tested for quality control.

3. Stored in warehouses until the age required for blending.

4. In some instances (mainly in the case of Whyte & Mackay, Invergordon, Robertson & Baxter and William Lawson) the ancient tradition of "marrying" will be carried out, where the malts are vatted together for a period separately from the grains. This, theoretically, is to help fuse all the constituent parts of the many different whiskies together to produce a more consistent product. Some blenders believe that the secret of a successful marrying process is to reduce the blend to 45–46 per cent ABV with demineralised water, before returning to well-used casks that will not further the ageing process.

5. The whiskies are "disgorged" or "troughed", whereby they are emptied to mix together prior to bottling. For smaller brands this can consist of just 50 casks of whisky. For Johnnie Walker Red, the world's top selling brand, ten tanker loads are used at a time.

6. The whisky is reduced down in strength to the desired alcohol content and chill filtered to remove some of the more solid oils that may produce clouding when cold. Unfortunately, this also removes some of the stronger flavours and aromas. Permitted colouring is also added in the form of caramel to ensure consistency of tone. In some cases, like Cutty Sark, no colouring is added at all.

CHAPTER FIVE

AN A–Z OF BRANDS

THE ANTIQUARY

It is always heartening to see a famous old blend in the hands of a small whisky company, as that is how it usually all started out. J. & W. Hardie Ltd may well be a subsidiary of Takara Shuzo – the Japanese owners of the Tomatin Distillery with strong links to the magnificent Ancient Age distillery in Frankfort, Kentucky – but until 1996 J. & W. Hardie was an entirely superfluous and invisible cog in the wheel of United Distillers. The Antiquary brand had been licensed over to William Sanderson; even the distillery under the Hardie name, Benromach, had been closed down.

Opposite
It was once common for local breweries to sport their own blended Scotch.

Now J. & W. Hardie have found independence again and, just as in the days when the brand was first launched in the late 1880s, the company is having to find new markets in order for it to thrive. Doubtless part of the plan was for Tomatin to have a blend to produce for, other than Big T. At the moment, however, UDV are contracted to produce the blend from their considerable stocks. Tomatin is, though, used as a base malt.

Most histories claim that J. & W. Hardie were established in 1861. The Antiquary label puts the date four years earlier. The fact is that no-one is exactly sure of the exact date when James Hardie set up his tea, wine and spirit merchants in Edinburgh. His sons John and William followed him into the business and began to concentrate more and more upon whisky and probably developed the blend at their Greenside Place shop and offices. Curiously, evidence points towards the Hardies naming the blend after a novel by Sir Walter Scott. In his book *The Antiquary* Scott writes about the Queensferry diligence which travelled each day from St Giles Cathedral, Edinburgh. The path it took passed the very home of one Mr James Hardie.

ABOUT THE BLEND
The Antiquary is heavier now than when I first tasted it in the late 70s. Before then the Speyside theme was always very dominant but now the slightly weightier background rumble of Tomatin is to be heard. Speyside does live on with the middle, focusing on the delights of Cragganmore in particular, but it is probably the honeyed Aberfeldy of Perthshire that helps give the blend such a magnificently rich start. Now, though, Bowmore acts as a gentle ballast. The grains are highly impressive and for that we must thank the unequalled quality of the late, lamented Cambus and some fine Port Dundas.

This superb twelve year old Scotch Whisky has been blended from a selection of Scotland's very finest malt and grain whiskies. It contains an unusually high percentage of malt which contributes to it's exceptionally smooth, long lingering after taste.

J & W HARDIE LTD
EDINBURGH
SCOTLAND

ESTABLISHED 1857

ESTABLISHED 1857

·THE·
ANTIQUARY
12 YEARS OLD
Superior Deluxe
SCOTCH WHISKY

DISTILLED, BLENDED & BOTTLED
IN SCOTLAND

40% vol 70cl ℮

Although the blend is still made under contract by UDV from their massive stocks, Hardie's managing director and master blender Jim Milne has had telling input into the style of the whisky.

NOSE Quite magnificent, uplifting start with a seductively grassy Speyside theme; fruity, unripened greengages and a tantalising smokiness which gives just the right weight against those lighter, malty notes. There is an oiliness that adds extra weight but the grain is extremely clean and does not make any effort to interfere with the delicate nature of this blend.

TASTE Initially fat, full and oily on the palate with a sweet Speyside-ish malt clinging to the mouth. Also, very early on the grain arrives hand-in-hand with the green apple-malt notes but as the flavours envelop the mouth the middle shows extensive and exclusive malt presence and is heavier than the nose might suggest. There is some lingering smokiness against the slightly flat barley and then a wave of cream toffee arrives with the grain.

FINISH Mainly grain here with a quick sliver of dark chocolate adding to the toffee. Some peat has just about clung on but that is all the malt you will find towards the medium-length finish. Soft and deft at the death but somehow just a little flat.

COMMENTS A delicate, rather delicious blend with very profound malt character and a quite superb nose. A genuine de luxe whisky, at its best between cool and warm when the full interaction of grain and malt is at play. Attractive although not imposingly complex. Perhaps because the blend got off to such a cracking start, re-enforced by the malty middle, the one disappointment lies with the finish, which ends too flat and quickly when really you want it to just carry on indefinitely.

THE BAILLIE NICOL JARVIE

The Antiquary is not alone as being a whisky coined from the pen of Sir Walter Scott. Another is the B.N.J. which, ironically, stems from Scott's work *Rob Roy*. And, yes, there is a whisky called Rob Roy, although produced by another company entirely.

The Baillie Nicol Jarvie was a magistrate in Scott's novel, a figment of the writer's imagination and a relative of the outlaw Rob Roy McGregor. However, the whisky bearing B.N.J.'s name today has virtually nothing in common with the blend which dates back to at least 1880 and was launched by Nicol Anderson, who were shortly to be taken over by the expanding MacDonald & Muir company. It was completely re-launched by Macdonald & Muir (now Glenmorangie Plc) in October 1994 and from that date has become indisputably one of the finest whiskies on the British market, to me a fabulous blend oozing rare subtlety and class.

It is thought that the B.N.J. name was first used as a whisky brand in around 1860 when it almost certainly would have been a mixture of Highland malt whiskies. It is highly unlikely grain played any part in the recipe. By the turn of the century it was a whisky which, with many others, found popularity in the mess tents of the Boer War.

However, the brand never took off as a major player in the whisky world. And although it will never match the likes of Dewar's, Bell's and Teacher's in terms of sales, it is a blend that has a tendency to win converts once tried. The label is one of my favourites, having faithfully maintained the simple character of a previous era – in this case late Victorian.

ABOUT THE BLEND

The press release that heralded the relaunch in October 1994 alluded to a "slight" formula change. That was something of an understatement. The whole blend is the brilliant creation of company blender John Smith. Where once the blend consisted of fifteen malts and two grains, now there are just nine malts and a single grain. The idea was to construct a premier dram sure in the knowledge that they would have sufficient supplies of these whiskies at the right ages for the foreseeable future. Naturally, the company's Glen Moray malt, one of my favourite blending whiskies, is used as the binding malt to cement the others together and some of those higher, lilting tones can be recognised as Glenmorangie at work. Remarkably the recipe works to a thumping ratio of 60 per cent malt (all First Divisioners), with some of the Glen Moray used 15-years-old, to 40 per cent grain. Smith made the brave decision to use only one grain, the firm and flavoursome North British. The result has been something that makes the average whisky connoisseur drool over.

NOSE Delicate and promising; about as sexy as a light whisky can be. An intriguing mixture of green, grassy young notes and some rich, honey oaken notes of age. And all the time the grain drives through to give a mouth-watering lightness perfectly balancing the subtle peats that give admirable depth. Memorable.

TASTE Every bit as mouth-watering on the palate as the nose suggests with some lemon tartness countering the rich maltiness and almost chewable grain. Perhaps the finest and most supremely constructed of all Scotland's lightweight whiskies.

FINISH Very long for such a fragile blend, with an astonishing depth of simple malt and toffee.

COMMENTS If I had to give a Top 5 listing of blended Scotch whisky, this is up there – and how! Every mouthful is a journey through the gamut of what Scotch mainland whisky has to offer. North British, because of its full ripeness of flavour, is a grain favoured by blenders who know how to make lightweight whiskies stand out. This is one such whisky. But perhaps it is that astonishing battle between the lighter, green under-ripe fruit notes and the aged malt which helps make this one of the world's truly most complex and highly desirable whiskies.

BALLANTINE'S

The extended family of Ballantine whiskies represents, with Johnnie Walker, the very best that Scottish distilling heritage has to offer. That may sound like something tapped from an advertising poster but it isn't. Because for me Ballantine's is what Scotch blended whisky is all about. Not only do you have a group of whiskies highly distinctive in style (occasional peatiness apart) individual to the Walker clan, but once again the history goes back to the days when blends were an entirely new art form experimented upon by people who knew only their customers' demands.

Indeed, the Ballantine name goes back a generation before then, to 1827. That was when the 18-year-old George Ballantine set up his modest grocer's in Cowgate, Edinburgh. By then this young man had already served a five-year apprenticeship to an Andrew Hunter. Significantly, Hunter had been not just a grocer but a spirit dealer. Soon George was dealing in whisky, too, not blended, but a rich spirit being brought in from the Highlands of Scotland. His success meant that within four years he had moved up-market to Candlemaker Row and five years later once again to South Bridge in the heart of the city. He had by now recognised where the bulk of his profit lay and now called his business "Wine Merchants and Grocers". The irony was, the higher up the social ladder you

travelled at that time, the less whisky you were
likely to sell to your clientele. But even so, whisky
still remained an invaluable part of his business.

George did not marry until he was into his
thirties but he had three sons, Archibald, George
and Daniel. As his sons grew into adulthood
George decided it was time for the Ballantine
name to spread. He set up a separate arm of the
business in Glasgow which he called George
Ballantine & Son while George Ballantine &
Sons continued as wine and tea merchants in the
up-market quarter of Edinburgh. In Glasgow old
George Ballantine still dealt in fine wine but
focused his business on whisky, a move that
proved to be a shrewd one. With his dealings in
the wine trade it meant that most of his whisky
matured in sherry casks, enabling a degree of
uniformity, an invaluable aid to the blender.
George the founder died in 1891 but his son
George and a grandson also called George
continued developing the Ballantine name and
brand through the Glasgow branch of the
business. Soon it had won royal warrants from
Queen Victoria and King Edward VII.

Yet by 1922 the Ballantine family had severed
all links with their famous brand. They had sold
both the Edinburgh and Glasgow businesses to
James Barclay and R. A. McKinlay three years
earlier and soon retired from the business.
Barclay and McKinlay formed George Ballantine
& Son into a limited company and immediately

This page
The streets of Edinburgh's Old Town, trading ground of merchants and grocers in the 19th century, were the birth place of many of the great Scotch blends.

expanded by purchasing James & George Stodart Ltd and the Old Smuggler brand.

It was a wonderfully prophetic brand for the Ballantine company to own. Under the Ballantine family, sales abroad had been very healthy. With Prohibition in America they were about to escalate beyond their wildest dreams. While the whisky could not be exported to America directly, Barclay ensured there was a roaring trade of the Ballantine brand to Nassau, a leading rum-running outpost, and Canada, the other main smuggling route. A number of photographs I have seen in America of customs agents smashing cases of bootleg whisky included Ballantine's among the horde. However, the contacts Barclay made during these dark days led once more to the takeover of the company. Toronto-based Hiram Walker-Gooderham and Worts, who owned the massive Canadian Club and Gooderham and Worts distilleries, were the next to acquire Ballantine, but such was their threat to the American market that they were forced to take action after they found it harder to purchase the Scotch grain whisky stocks required to keep the Ballantine sales booming. Harry Hatch at Hiram Walker began making sure whisky stocks would be forthcoming. First he acquired the Miltonduff and Glenburgie distilleries in Speyside. Then, famously, he decided to build his own grain plant in retaliation after the chairman of the Distillers Company, Sir Henry

Ross, kept him continuously waiting for a meeting to discuss grain availability.

The imposing Dumbarton grain distillery was built specifically to furnish the Ballantine brand with all the grain it needed as Hiram Walker looked to make it Scotland's single largest export whisky. It was completed in 1938 but the war years put paid to plans to send millions of cases each year into the United States. Dumbarton still today supplies the bulk of the grain whisky used for Ballantine's blends, although the little Lowland malt distillery built in its shadow,

Above

US Prohibition officers raid a store of bootleg whisky. In this era, Ballantine's already-healthy American exports rocketed beyond their wildest dreams.

Inverleven, has been silent almost thoughout the 1990s and is unlikely to play any further role in the Ballantine Finest blend.

Today Ballantine's is part of Allied Domecq, owners of Hiram Walker. Each year some five million cases are sold throughout the world, making it the third best-selling Scotch. In Europe, the other direction in which Hatch had been looking for exports to go, sales are nothing short of phenomenal.

ABOUT THE BLEND

When the trend is towards blends with fewer constituent parts it is always a delight to find a whisky like Ballantine's: no less than 57 malts are found in the recipe. Naturally enough those owned by Allied, such as Miltonduff and Glenburgie, have pivotal roles, as does the mouth-watering maize grain from Dumbarton.

BALLANTINE'S FINEST

NOSE Quintessential blended Scotch whisky: an intriguing mixture of aloof grains and fruity, grassy notes cemented with something deliciously peaty. Imagine how a great all-round blend should nose, and this is just about it.

TASTE Initially light and sweet with the grains, clean and slightly oaky, driving through first then an immediate shock wave of peat. The more easy-going, chewy malts arrive third but are thinned out by a resurgence of drier grain.

FINISH Medium length with lots of toffee, cocoa and oak carried on the grain. Just a little peat hangs around to give a weightier send-off than first seems possible.

COMMENTS This is quite excellent whisky; nothing like as complex as an older Ballantine's but at once intriguingly solid and translucent to the palate. There are signs that it is just a shade lighter than, say, four or five years ago and not quite so sweet. But really lovely stuff, nonetheless, and beautifully balanced: hence its all-round appeal to the world's palates.

FAMILY BLENDS
BALLANTINE'S GOLD SEAL 12-YEAR-OLD
Slightly similar on the nose to Royal Blue, except for an earthier base. Still impressive elements of the highest quality Canadian lurking in there. Fatter, oilier and infinitely more complex than Royal Blue with myriad malty facets fighting for

top spot. The grain comes and goes throughout and as it fades the malt, with a more smoky constant, makes the taste buds work overtime. Only at the finish does the grain dominate with a hint of burnt sugar. Magnificently lip-smacking, full-bloodied stuff. A much more impressive and satisfying blend than Royal Blue.

BALLANTINE'S ROYAL BLUE 12-YEAR-OLD

The nose is nothing short of mouth-watering with an unusual mixture of apple-fresh Speyside notes and old Canadian (probably the result of well-aged grain). There is a vaguely honeyed sweetness in there too but on the palate the first to show are rich smoky notes that had kept the lowest of profiles on the nose. However, as the nose implies, there is a brief mouth-watering explosion of grassy malts then a wonderful tail-off of complex grain malt dovetailing with Speyside still holding the upper hand. The peat lingers on the finish but it's mainly the treacle/ caramel-roasty grain that hangs on longest.

BALLANTINE'S 15-YEAR-OLD

Thinner and grainier than both the 12-year-old and even Ballantine's Finest. There is just a hint of pine adding to the freshness and is the youngest Ballantine to show peppers on the nose. A slight oiliness is evident, not unlike crushed sunflower seeds. To taste is at first rather warming, spicy and alcohol-hot. There is a wave of sweet barley but this is soon overwhelmed by a return of the grain. For me the least sophisticated, most grain-dominant of all the Ballantine brands – the only one I am not stuck on.

BALLANTINE'S 17-YEAR-OLD

ABOUT THE BLEND

It is only during the final stages of writing this book that I discovered just how many blenders share my view about this cracking de luxe whisky. Because it is a rival blend to those one or two fellow-admirers I will not say just exactly who they are, but as blenders rarely get round to tasting a great number of the opposition's wares, it is doubly gratifying to learn that fellow-professionals regard this the finest Ballantine's they have tasted. Despite the great age, some forty malts have still been mustered together, a remarkable feat. And once more it is the usual Allied gang of malts and grains that lead the way.

NOSE Subtle echoes of lavender and mint balance beautifully with equally subtle peat and grain. Everything is cleverly understated yet the overall effect is quite enormous. An extremely clever nose, beguiling and wonderfully sexy. Best at hand temperature.

TASTE Although silky on the palate, thanks to a wonderful sweet, oily sheen that coats the mouth, there are sufficient pepper and grain notes to remind the palate that much is going on. The sweetish maltiness is of awesome complexity with clean grassy notes mingling superbly with peat smoke and an encroaching oakiness. Enormous with wave upon wave of intense barley sugar and peat but never overwhelming. Again, at hand temperature it hits the palate with great intensity.

FINISH Oaky but never sappy with delightful chocolate notes harmonising with a some late sweet raisins and hazelnut.

COMMENTS One of my favourite blends and one of about half a dozen I am most likely to choose from before retiring to bed. (Not a bad one to start the day with, either.) Where the 15-year-old doesn't quite manage to harmonise, the 17-year-old is an exhibition in the art of blending. There seems to be a little bit of everything and always in the right order. If it does have a drawback, the oakyness can, after the fourth or fifth mouthful, become quite intense. But that perhaps help demonstrate just how delicate this big whisky is. Truly classic.

FAMILY BLENDS

BALLANTINE'S 18-YEAR-OLD

A sharper, nippier dram on the nose than the 17-year-old but with some tangerine and soft bourbon and freshly cut new bread notes thrown in; to taste is initially softer, sweeter and silkier on the palate but does not pan out with such complexity as the 17. Also the cocoa-bitter oak from the grain is perhaps just a little too bombastic. Perhaps too dry on the finish to make this a truly great whisky

BALLANTINE'S 21-YEAR-OLD

ABOUT THE BLEND

This must be good. Allied have actually invested in a cork stopper, something sadly lacking from the younger Ballantine blends. Indeed, they have gone the whole hog: the whisky is contained in a stylish cobalt blue Wade porcelain decanter. I don't know for sure just how many malts are included, but as the 30-year-old has in the region of thirty-six to thirty-eight, the number here must still be high.

NOSE Quite wondrous. There are certainly traces of bourbon, as one would expect, but they are minimal and sink below a sea of fresh malt. Beautifully balanced in being both sweet and dry almost simultaneously. This most subtle of noses offers a hint of pepper and smoke but it is the refined citric fruitiness which really impresses.

TASTE Moderately fat on the mouth and soft – then *whoosh*! The palate is hit by an assortment of riches spearheaded by gentle peats and almost chewable barley grist. Astonishing and at its best when taken by the mouthful and kept there for a good ten seconds.

FINISH The grain had kept a respectful distance but came in as a cream toffee sweetness begins to fade. Even so this is really top quality grain, as rounded as a pebble on a beach. Amazingly long and impressive with the peat hanging on to the very death.

COMMENTS You can visit the Louvre and the Tate but even there you will find few works of art to match this one. The balance is quite breathtaking. Throughout there is an agreeable sweetness yet never does it become even remotely cloying. The sweetness is always on a knife-edge with some darker, peaty, grainy notes keeping a close watch. Finally, at the end, the grain has its say but does so in a cultured way. Intoxicating stuff, but mainly for the dizzy heights it reaches as a whisky. Brilliant.

FAMILY BLENDS
BALLANTINE'S 30-YEAR-OLD

It is hard to believe that a blend of such great age could be shoved into a screw-cap bottle with not even a hint of writing telling you anything about the whisky, but that is the bizarre case of Ballantine's 30. I know Ardbeg has gone into this in the past, because I was once at the distillery when some 30-year-old from that magnificent distillery was carted off to be added to it. There is peat on the nose but, like the 25-year-old Putachieside, the main notes are of old bourbony cognac. Sheer velvet on the palate with an agreeable mixture of sweet and sour notes. Ultra-ripe plums, under-ripe cherries and hot chillies intermingle on the taste buds and some chalky oak finishes off the proceedings. The fine bitter chocolate comes as standard. Full marks for getting a blend this age to last the course.

BELL'S

Ask anyone in Britain to name a whisky and the chances are that Bell's will be the first name to come to mind, irrespective of whether the person is a whisky drinker or not. This is not surprising as this brand represents one of the great post-war success stories in Scotch whisky.

Yet, as is so often the case, the brand and company can be traced back to very humble beginnings. The original Arthur Bell was a man who seemed in many ways to personify the Victorian businessman and business values. His introduction to whisky came as a young salesman for Sandeman of Perth, a relative of the Port family. That was in 1840, the year of the world's first Penny Post. When in 1851 he struck out on his own with James Roy, a colleague from Sandeman's, the firm became known as Roy & Bell, although it was not long before Roy retired. Bell had learnt early on, even before grain whiskies were used, that vatting malts together produced a whisky more desirable than single malts. When someone wrote to him to discover just why his whisky was so good, he replied: "I do not usually give the mixture of my whiskies, but may mention that the best is made in Banffshire's Glenlivet district and the other is Pitlochry and Stirlingshire whiskies." It is likely that the Pitlochry distillery was Blair Athol, which would have been fitting, as it was bought by the company in 1933 to become their first distillery.

Left
*Old Arthur Bell,
thrifty
philanthropist,
in many ways
personified
conservative
Victorian
business values.*

By then Arthur Bell had been dead for thirty-three years. He had been a remarkable man, renowned for watching every single penny that entered and exited his company's accounts, yet generous to a fault for providing for his extended family out of duty and fondness hidden under a blanket of Victorian impassivity. His son who carried the business forward, also Arthur Bell but known as "AK", was every bit as outgoing as his father had been reserved. Old Arthur had not

been entirely without vision: he is believed to have been the first blender to employ an agent in London and led the way for the standardisation of bottle sizes. But under his command no advertising was permitted and using Bell as a brand name was strictly forbidden. In 1904, however, "AK" commissioned the famous old "Curler" label that was slapped on bottles of his whisky, complete with the Bell's name. Like today's label it gave the year of establishment as 1825, which is when the Sandeman business was formed, rather than Bell's.

The buying of the ancient Blair Athol distillery – which in 1998 celebrated its 200th anniversary

– along with Dufftown, all part of their takeover of the P. Mackenzie Co. of Edinburgh, was swiftly followed by the purchase of Inchgower. Over the years Bladnoch was also acquired and Pittyvaich built next to Dufftown. The investment of the latter two distilleries came about when sales of Bell's began soaring through the roof. The company had gone public in 1949, by which time there was no longer any Bell serving on the board. However, it was in the 1970s that sales begun their extraordinary upward surge with their distilleries increasing output nearly 300 per cent over a decade. In 1985 the company was taken over by Guinness, who two years later also acquired the giant DCL. Under United Distillers the blend was re-launched as an 8-year-old in 1994.

ABOUT THE BLEND

For some years before the company was taken over by what is now UDV, Bell's reputation plummeted and not without good cause. The demand for the blend outstripped supply of malt from Bell's badly neglected distilleries and quality was affected. When Bell's were taken over, the blend immediately had far more and better malts for inclusion. Some drinkers have stayed away, remembering the bad old days of the late 70s and early 80s. That is their loss because the whisky, now an 8-year-old, has changed beyond recognition, although its traditional malts, Blair

Athol, Inchgower and Dufftown, are finding their way back into the blend as the malt produced there has improved. The roughest of the old guard, Pittyvaich, is missing. Malt comprises just in excess of 35 per cent of the blend and Linkwood takes a starring role. Caol Ila adds some weighty ballast, although the Islay content has dropped over the years.

NOSE Heather-honeyed and ethereally light. The grains offer a cutting cleanness and allow the malts room to play. Hardly any real smoky depth, this nose depends on the unmistakable refined complexity of some supreme malts, with Speyside and Perthshire playing the dominating role.

TASTE An extraordinary introduction of finely balanced malt and grain from the off. Impressive because the grain is given a key role of lightening and thinning the malt intensity. The malts are every bit as complex as the nose suggests: there is a slight raisiny fruitiness amid the clean barley, mouth-watering fresh grass and vague sweetish walnut nuttiness. But this never dominates as the toffee-d grain cuts in, time and time again.

FINISH Just a faint trace of smoke adds some late weight to the blend but it is the clean grain vanilla plus some uncluttered maltiness that finishes the journey.

COMMENTS A highly satisfying whisky that is about as far removed from the old Bell's as you could imagine. Where the old Bell's was smoky and grimy, this is about as clean as Scotch gets, but has a subtle, bristling complexity. Intriguingly there has been no attempt to try and hide the dampening effect of the grain – indeed, quite the reverse.

FAMILY BLENDS
BELL'S 12-YEAR-OLD
Beautifully presented in a chunky, bell-shaped bottle, this blend has retained the now trademark Bell's laid-back character but offers on the nose an even more intense honey and just a slightly deeper smoke to counter-balance. Fatter on the palate and initially sweeter, the malt has far bigger intensity before the warming spices and grain take command. The finish is comparatively thin. Oddly, not quite as complex as the standard Bell's, although medium-weighted, delicious stuff nonetheless.

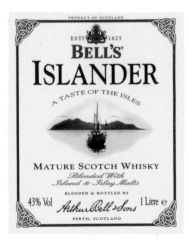

BELL'S ISLANDER

Spicy, peppery and lively on the nose. The tingle also contains controlled peatyness that is nowhere to be found on the other Bell's. To taste, this is much maltier throughout and offers undisguised Hebridean depth and chewyness with a Talisker-esque buzz. The grains remain clean and add a degree of toffee sweetness that fits in with the roasty, malt peatyness beautifully. A distinctly satisfying dram which is dangerously moreish.

BEN ALDER

This is just one of a number of blends from the independent blenders and distillers Gordon & MacPhail. Based in Speyside's capital city, Elgin, G&M are world renowned for their excellent and extensive range of single malt whiskies. During the 60s and 70s when single malt whisky was so hard to come by, whisky lovers always found relief by finding a Gordon & MacPhail stockist carrying the famous Connoisseur's Choice range.

But with single malt whiskies now so easy to find, it is worth remembering that G&M also blend whisky too. The five listed below are what I personally consider to be the best of their large blend portfolio and when looking through a selection of their whiskies, or visiting their old shop, you will be rewarded by trying at least one of these brands.

Like so many of the more famous blending names, the company started off as a grocer's and tea, wine and spirit merchant's. That was in 1895 and soon the two partners, James Gordon and John MacPhail, were gaining a reputation for the quality of their fine malt whiskies. Serving that north-eastern corner of the Highlands there was then little call for blended Scotch, although they still produced some for their expanding markets in London and abroad. One of the young boys first employed by the new business was John Urquhart who, after twenty years of learning every aspect of the business, became a junior partner on MacPhail's retirement in 1915. Two weeks later the

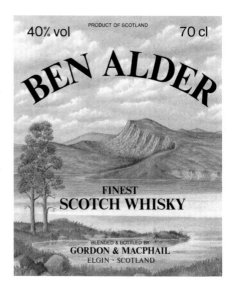

firm's guiding light, James Gordon, died suddenly and John Urquhart took over as the senior partner.

The business has remained in the Urquhart family ever since and the shop still runs from those first premises opened in South Street on the 24 May 1895. The warehousing and blending is now carried out at new premises at the edge of the town and it is Ian Urquhart, grandson of John Urquhart, who carries out the blending.

Some of the brands, like Spey Cast, date back to the 1890s when James Gordon was blender – and the timelessness of the label reflects this. Ben Alder, originally called Dew of Ben Alder, is also thought to be a Gordon creation. The most famous brand of them all, though, is Old Orkney. This blend was created in the 1980s when it was discovered no-one owned the name of the famous single malt linked with the old Stromness distillery on Orkney that fell silent in 1928. After a gap of over fifty years one of the most famous whisky names was resurrected. History repeated itself during 1998 when the company brought the silent Benromach distillery, which they purchased in 1993, back on stream. That will be finding its way into their blends before it is launched as a single malt.

About the blend

With grains aged around the three-year mark and malts twice that age with undoubtedly something almost ancient finding its way in there as well, this is a malt that sticks to a Speyside character but offers something else besides. The malts seem to be in the 35–40 per cent region and the two grains used, Invergordon and North British, guarantee a good soft-firm balance.

NOSE A beautifully crafted blend on the nose, showing evidence of whiskies of good age and dexterity. Some younger citrus tones lighten the main honey-vanilla theme.

TASTE No less delicate on the palate, starting off as soft and silky-malty as any you might find, then a brilliant beguiling build-up of spice reaches a crescendo. The lemony notes remain throughout. Brilliantly complex.

FINISH Those peppery notes linger on and are met by some developing honey (very unusual of a finish) and then more oak that again suggests some good age for a blend of unspecified ancestry.

COMMENTS One of the great blends of Scotland, the taste buds can never tire of the clever spiciness that builds so well. The kind of blend that once you start, you find very difficult to put down. First class with honours.

FAMILY BLENDS
Frasers Supreme
Smokier aroma than most from Gordon & Macphail, being slightly roasty and crisp, and on the palate one of the most complex of all the G&M blends thanks to some astute use of the grain to interact with the sweet, nutty malt and hints of peat.

Old Orkney "OO"
One of the most famous turn-of-the-century names in malt whisky has been transformed into a blend. The Stromness Distillery on Orkney, one of the smallest in the world, failed in 1928. After the turn of the century it had tried to win converts to malts, and looked for the London area in particular to embrace the "OO" slogan but custom was not forthcoming. In this blend that carries the proud old name there is lovely use of grain to lighten the citric, malty notes on the nose. Beautifully soft on the palate and, like Ben Alder, builds up in spiciness. Similar in structure to that great blend but without the intensity.

The Spey Cast 12-years-old

A firm, sweet nose with bananas, gooseberries, custard and spice. Excellent early mouth-feel: fat and immediately spicy with excellent build-up of intense malt and soft, Canadian-style toffee-ed grain.

Ubique

Fabulous nose, showing good age, a hint of bourbon vanilla, a dash of honey, toffee apple and old polished leather.

Immediately voluptuous on the palate with that honey staying deep and rich with a sprinkle of demerara sugar and much deeper, vaguely smoky, deep fruity notes. A classic, only just eclipsed by Ben Alder, but seemingly lasts for ever.

BLACK BOTTLE

While Chivas and Catto became internationally famous names from Aberdonian beginnings, another native blending company of that beautiful city tended to keep their distinctive brand as something for the locals to savour. That was until 1959 when Gordon Graham & Co. sold their name and their much-prized but little-known brand Black Bottle to Schenley, owners of Long John. It ended eighty years of proud independence for the erstwhile tea importers who had created in Black Bottle a brand which was synonymous with the Scottish north-east, as I discovered in the early 1980s when I first began spending months in Fraserburgh, Peterhead and finally Aberdeen where I was introduced to my future father-in-law. No matter whom I met, every conversation about Scotch seemed to end with: "Have you tried the Black Bottle yet?" In its Long John days the blend was pretty awful whisky, perhaps ruined by too much unforgiving Strathclyde and not enough top quality malt. When it became part of the Allied Domecq empire the whisky was completely regenerated and became unquestionably one of the finest in Scotland. In 1995 the brand passed to Highland Distilleries, who have embarked on a brave and frankly brilliant programme to make it the peaty full-flavoured alter ego to their Famous Grouse brand.

Opposite
The
Bunnahabhain
virtually
unpeated Islay
malt contributes
to the Black
Bottle blend.

THE HIGHLAND DISTILLERIES COMPANY P.L.C.

1984

BUNNAHABHAIN

ISLAY

1900

ABOUT THE BLEND

There have been subtle changes since Highland Distilleries bought the brand. Now all seven Islay whiskies are represented in this blend (Port Ellen being the absentee) with Laphroaig maintaining a lofty position and Ardbeg adding untold complexity. However, it is the virtually unpeated Islay, Bunnahabhain, which is the biggest representative, adding a salty tang. Among the non-Islays Glenrothes adds a sweet maltiness, while of the grains Strathclyde holds its historic place but is more than supported by the quite polarised North British and Girvan: quite a mix. This is far removed from the days before Gordon Graham & Co. lost independence in 1959. In the last few years before then their whisky relied on a honeyed, estery theme slightly similar to Jamaican pot still rum, but it was very much lighter with the soft grains dominating in tandem with Speyside malt and a heathery background. Peat appeared at a premium in the blend which remained, however, deceptively intense. The whisky today has turned 180 degrees.

NOSE Earthy, smoky, pungent and distinctly salty. Quite dry with good grain firmness but it is the peat that enjoys the lion's share of the character.

TASTE Sweetens immediately on the palate with a quite brilliant array of Islay-iodine and smoke notes. Quite beautiful cocoa-oak dryness clashes head-on with some sweeter peat notes and unmistakable Speyside. Highly complex and unashamedly islandy in style but there is just a hint of something fruity – mainly over-ripe plums.

FINISH Long, lingering salt and drying peat with a developing vanilla intensity and tingling spices.

COMMENTS The new bottle makes the claim: "Finest Scotch Whisky with a Heart of Islay" and they are not kidding. Curiously, the nose is more closed than in its Allied days, with not quite the same honeyed softness that was a trademark of the original, independent blend of forty years ago. But flavour-wise the current Black Bottle wins handsomely with a full-bodied, muscular blend that is as chewy as a peat bog and as islandy as the screech of a seagull. A brave, uncompromising and truly glorious whisky.

BLACK BOTTLE 10-YEAR-OLD

A stonking, full-blooded blend that has done the unthinkable – it has restricted the malts to Islays only. This includes a fair percentage of Bunnahabhain (some up to 14-year-old) which means there is a malty respite from the delicious havoc caused by the Laphroaig and Bowmore. But all seven working Islay distilleries are in there, to varying degrees. The nose shows salt-and-pepper intensity with seductive peat reek and to taste is chewy and smoky with a malt-grainy bite. The finish shows licorice and coffee and is almost endless: a delight for Islayphiles; a supreme but no means insurmountable challenge for those who haven't made it that far yet.

BLACK COCK

One of a number of blends from Burn Stewart directed at the export market, notably France. Another blend I have been known to occasionally take to parties where once, memorably, it sat alongside Black Bush and VAT 69. Not the finest whisky from the Burn Stewart stable, with a big grainy attack on the nose and palate. But there is sufficient malt to make for a busy, mouth-watering mouthful with some sweet grain and both grassy and earthy Highland malt having their moments of supremacy. Not bad at all.

BLACK WATCH

Marketing people are convinced that a whisky with the name "Black" in it is sure to be a winner: doubtless because of the success of Buchanan's Black and White and Johnnie Walker Black Label. Hence we have, bought recently by Highland Distilleries at some cost, Black Bottle, and other brands in no particular order including Black Dog, Black Top, Black Prince and even Black Cock. The latest is Black Watch, which until 1997 had been known throughout the world as Seagram's popular, low-budget dram 100 Pipers.

ABOUT THE BLEND
Little if any information is volunteered on this blend. Let's just say that the grain plays an important role.

NOSE Extremely light with lots of grain and citrus. Flattened slightly by a hint of cream-toffee caramel.

TASTE Quite fiery from the start with a solid, uncompromising young grain presence. Malt is present but totally lacking in complexity and depth and little more substantial than a layer of dust over the grain.

FINISH Caramel and vanilla.

COMMENTS I didn't much like 100 Pipers and I can't say I'm much of a fan of this, either. The only whisky in this book to make me cough while tasting. And that was before I swallowed. A real rough and ready whisky which in its favour is clean and has no off-notes. But the caramel is just too dominant. My old mate Wallace Milroy would probably describe this as a case of the "fiery dancers". I have never quite known exactly what that means, but it would sum this whisky up perfectly.

BLACK & WHITE

The Black & White brand, which has only just been restored to British whisky shelves, has remained throughout the 20th century one of the world's favourite and most easily recognisable blends. This would have brought a smile to the great James Buchanan who spent a lifetime pouring what energy his ill health allowed him to

CLASSIC BLENDED SCOTCH

"Didn't you call for 'Black & White'?"

More and more people are calling for "BLACK &
WHITE" because of its fine flavour and character. It is
a firm favourite with the new generation as well as
the old. "BLACK & WHITE" is a most effective
stimulant at all times, and is especially helpful in
these days of stress and strain. It relieves fatigue
and renews your energy. Call for it by name—

"BLACK&WHITE"

"It's the Scotch!"

C.J.L. (b)

98

muster into building a whisky brand of unfailing stature. Buchanan may have been born in Canada and brought up in Northern Ireland, but with a Scottish name and Scottish parents there was little doubting where his future lay. At the age of 15 he landed in Scotland and began working in shipping as an office boy. By the turn of the century he would be heavily involved in shipping again: it was the only means by which he could get his famous whiskies to their markets across the globe.

He had begun in the whisky business in 1879 as the London agent for Charles Mackinlay, one of the earliest established blenders. By the mid-1880s he had raised enough money to set out on his own. He had already become well known for his lively and engaging personality and soon he was winning customers over. He first managed to get his whisky served in the bars of Westminster, thereby launching his House of Commons blend. This brand evolved into "Black and White" on account of the white label beaming from the black bottle. Such was his success that he built the Glentauchers distillery in Speyside to guarantee malt supplies for his blend and although it still produces one of Speyside's firmest and finest whiskies it is today owned by Allied Domecq, which is ironic because Black and White is today a product of rivals United Distillers and Vintners. James Buchanan had, with Dewar and Johnnie Walker, formulated the

Opposite

Its instantly recognisable brand image helped establish Black & White as a favourite household name.

top league of the independent companies competing against DCL and to strengthen their hand Buchanan merged with Dewar in 1915 to form Scotch Whisky Brands, although a few years later, perhaps wishing to keep their famous names to the fore, this became Buchanan-Dewar. However, in 1923 the inevitable occurred when they, with Johnnie Walker, became part of DCL.

ABOUT THE BLEND

Dalwhinnie heads the list of malts used for out-and-out flavouring and is evident on the nose, with Clynelish and Royal Brackla adding malty support. Both UDV grains, Port Dundas and Cameronbridge, are used but, with around 60–65 per cent grain being present, other patent stills are employed as well.

NOSE Shows all the signs of a grain-led blend with the malt adding negligible weight. Even so, this still offers something gentle and attractive: there is not a single off or discordant note. A little heather-peatyness acts as a perfect foil to one of the lightest noses offered by UDV.

TASTE Sombre and unbelievably low-key at first, the middle does perk up with a slow build-up of, at first, grainy toffee then more profound, momentarily sharpish maltiness. Remains moderately sweet thoughout but the grain does proffer a countering dryness. Excellent balance.

FINISH Carries on at the same slow pace with now some phenolic spiciness tingling the taste buds a little. The toffee continues and is replaced by gentle vanillins and chalky oak.

COMMENTS This is quality although unexciting whisky. Every single whisky being used here is as clean and precise as you could wish for. Perhaps some characters do cancel each other out so that complexity is kept to a minimum. But this is a gentle, pleasing dram that is nothing like as rich, fruity, smoky and bold as it was a few years ago.

BLACK PRINCE

This became one of the first brands bought by the distillers and blenders Burn Stewart after their management buy-out in 1991. Since acquiring it from Bols, they have turned a pretty average blend into something worth finding. The brand, named after the 14th-century son of King Edward III, was launched by the Dutch distillers Henkes and was later blended by their British subsidiary Nordren McCall of London before the brand returned to Holland when it was sold to Bols. Always an export brand, it is today found principally in France, Portugal, Taiwan and Paraguay.

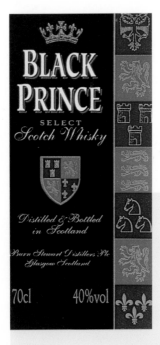

ABOUT THE BLEND

A very healthy 35 per cent content has imperious Imperial heading the full-blooded contingent with Caol Ila guaranteeing weight and length. Home-grown Deanston helps lighten it a little though the grain, this being a Burn Stewart blend, has a stiff backbone thanks to the Girvan–North British duet.

NOSE Fantastically lively and peppery: not a nose that sits on the fence. There are hints of honey sweetness, toffee and seriously characterful grain. A whisky which jumps out at you demanding to be noticed.

TASTE Equally explosive on the palate, with first a good spicy start and then a thick blanket of honeyed malt. Some toffee caramel reaches the middle plus a touch of apricot and coconut. The grain is also very active, biting at the taste buds with playful nips.

FINISH Lots of vanilla and smoke on this long finish, and as the grain begins to kick in there is chocolate topping. There is a sweet edge to the death, but some intriguing bitterness from the grain to counter.

COMMENTS Wow! A fighting, charismatic blend that perfectly matches the character after whom it was named. This is a whisky lover's blend: for those who look for something beyond "smooth" and "mellow" but look for a whisky with an intent. In this case it is to give the taste buds a good duffing-up with an almost spectacular display of spice, smoke and honey. Fabulous whisky.

FAMILY BLENDS
BLACK PRINCE 12 YEARS OLD

A more civilised dram with an outstandingly beautiful, very slightly bourbony nose as soft and docile as the younger version is lively. The honeyed theme continues and the black pepper, although there, is more restrained. For some reason, though, on the palate the grains are more dominant than the standard Black Prince and there is much less flavour complexity. But this remains a genuinely impressive dram with a strange hint of strawberries on the finish. Very cultured and well balanced.

BLACK PRINCE OVER 20 YEARS

Drier and oakier aroma with less honey and more vanilla. On the palate, though, the delicate

sweetness clings unwaveringly to the palate and offers Javan coffee and blackcurrant on the palate. Like the nose, the finish is drier than its stablemates, but the oak is vanilla-rich and chalky although this is enlivened by a wave of boiled apple and fresh, green malt. A superbly weighted, Premier League whisky from first to last.

BLUE HANGER

A colossal whisky from Berry Bros. & Rudd, the little-known star of a highly impressive range of blends from the famous old wine and spirit merchant in St. James's Street, London (*see* Cutty Sark). This is the only blend I can think of named directly after a customer, in this case a rather strange dandy dressed all in blue who used to frequent the then new premises in the late 17th century. His peculiar figure is depicted on the label.

ABOUT THE BLEND

This is at an unusually high strength of 45.6 per cent ABV and as such has kept, even after chill filtering, many of the long-chain fatty acids that guarantee extra depth and richness of flavour. But that is not all: the last vatting of this little known blend was some five years ago, so although the original whiskies used had ranged from eight to twelve years, they have been in cask not just marrying but maturing for five extra years. The result is perhaps one of the finest

blends you are likely to find today. Being a Berry
Bros. product, the blending has been carried out
by Robertson & Baxter and you can be assured
that Glen Rothes, Highland Park, Bunnahabhain
and North British play key roles in the character
profile: just check out the saltiness.

NOSE Brilliant nose: salty sea-breeze, malty with excellent
grain prickle and again as with most Berry Bros. whisky there is
that fabulous bitter-sweet balance with just the faintest trace of
marmalade and honey.

TASTE On the palate there is an awesome depth and
oiliness; the whisky is big yet the lightness means the complexity
is remarkably high. Few whiskies come close to matching the
bitter-sweet balance: the spices range from white pepper to hints
of paprika and the maltiness is thick enough to cut through.

FINISH An extra layer of oak arrives, suggesting some very
decent age and some delicious grain lightness thins the salty
malt. Fabulous.

COMMENTS It had been a few years since I last tasted Blue
Hanger and it certainly wasn't like this in the past. Of all the
250+ current blends I tasted in the final stages of writing this
book, this was the biggest and most delicious surprise.
Uncompromising, multifaceted whisky of the highest order,
although in short supply. If you are ever in London, always make
sure you come home with a bottle of this, one of the finest blends
you are ever likely to savour. Or you might find it at the newly
opened Berry Bros. & Rudd shop at Heathrow. Forget single
malts: a glass of this and you will be hooked on blends for life.

BUCHANAN'S
(*see* Black and White)

BUCHANAN'S 12-YEAR-OLD

ABOUT THE BLEND
The younger version boasts an amazing malt content, something approaching the 50 per cent mark. Dalwhinnie leads the way among the malts and is represented in the honey-effect while Talisker and Caol Ila add spice and weight respectively. There is also good use of sherry cask, and Glendullan helps with some extra Speyside depth. There is a fraction more grain in the 18-year-old but the sherry cask content remains high and the super-clean Speysider Aultmore allows the more intense Dalwhinnie and Glendullan to show impressively.

NOSE What an extraordinary and quite classic balance between grassy Speyside lightness, Perthshire-style honey sweetness, understated peaty smoke and bourbony oak-carrying grain. A subject lesson for every student of whisky to study.

TASTE A blend that gets the juices running thanks to those extremely clean Speyside attributes linking up with something a bit darker and heather-honeyed. But what sets this apart is the clarity of everything that flits around the mouth. Tons of heather-honeyed spice and peat. Although outwardly light, has massive depth on which to chew upon. There is also a very satisfying grain bite.

FINISH Long, honeycombed and soft vanilla and milk chocolate. Medium to long – could be longer.

COMMENTS Buchanan 12, next to the subtler Johnnie Walker Black, has always been the blend I admired most and thoroughly loved drinking. The amazing news is that it just gets better and better. This is much more complex and confident than it was just four or five years ago with the honey playing a more telling factor. Perhaps the only blend around that can give Black Label a real run for its money. A genius of a whisky.

FAMILY BLENDS
JAMES BUCHANAN AGED 18 YEARS
The dark horse of the family, quite literally. James Buchanan made his name on his black and white brand and in colour this is black to the 12-year-old's white. The nose enjoys none of the 12-year-old's complexity but the sherry and peat notes do get along nicely. The palate, however, is a different matter. Unbelievably intense, there is all the richness of a Melton Mowbray Hunting Cake and loads of raisins and nuts accompanying a slightly burnt effect. The finish is smoky and lingering. All round, one of the sweetest and

deepest blends on the market anywhere in the world. For some, this will be one of the greatest whiskies they will ever experience. For me, the sherry is just a little too much and the sweetness needs lightening by the grain. But there is no detracting from a profound and highly delicious blend.

CADENHEAD'S PUTACHIESIDE

It seemed that during the 19th century if your surname began with "C" and you were born in or around Aberdeen, there was a very good chance you would end up as a whisky merchant. First of all there were, of course, Chivas and later Catto. In between came William Cadenhead, who actually predated Catto by two decades, having started business in 1842.

The label of Putachieside brand depicts that ancient area of Aberdeen, behind the wonderful Prince of Wales pub where Marks & Spencer now stands. That was the where the Cadenhead business started and ended. The Cadenhead family died out at the same time in the mid-60s that the old shop was demolished. In the picture is the Wallace Tower, which has now been removed to another part of the city.

Cadenhead has for many years been under the auspices of J. A. Mitchell, owners of Springbank distillery who bought the aged

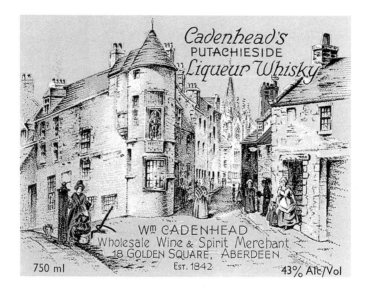

stocks. Although the business has been closed in Aberdeen it thrives in two up-market locations: the Royal Mile in Edinburgh and at Covent Garden in London. Cadenhead were famed throughout Aberdeen for their rum perhaps even more so than their whisky. And while Cadenhead still retain some of the finest rum stocks in Britain, their name has become a by-word for high quality single malts bottled direct from the barrel: unfiltered and at full strength. Putachieside is their top-range blend to match their malts.

CADENHEAD'S PUTACHIESIDE 12-YEAR-OLD

ABOUT THE BLEND
It is worth noting that with neither of these blends did I use my spittoon, as is usually the case.

NOSE A stonking nose, easily one of the most complex of any blend in the world. Here are just a few of things you may find in no particular order: salt, myrrh, sawdust, acacia honey, figs, coconut, freshly ground barley malt, apples.

TASTE The taste buds are entirely over-run by a flavoursome re-enactment of the aroma. The middle is also enormously spicy and throughout, amid the mouth-watering ripe apples and spring grass, there is a vein of smoke running right through it all.

FINISH Just about endless. The delicate spices become a little more herbal and the oak begins to offer vanilla and toffee.

COMMENTS What can you say? Breathtaking whisky, easily in the top five blends you are likely to find. In some ways it is almost too intense and you need more grain to come in and relieve the pleasure. It's a bit like being in agony from laughing too much. A whisky you must try in order to see what I mean: otherwise it's nearly impossible to describe.

CADENHEAD'S PUTACHIESIDE 25-YEAR-OLD
Massive bourbon character from some obviously ancient grains sit comfortably with the saltier malt tones. Something to be appreciated by Wild Turkey 12-year-old lovers. Amazingly sweet and silky. Rather than tasting like Scotch it has taken on a more ancient bourbon and brandy character. A superb experience: nothing short of a one-off. But as a Scotch the 12-year-old is the better act. Little surprise they use the old and nearly lost term of Liqueur Whisky.

FAMILY BLENDS
Campbeltown Loch
This whisky has radically changed in the last fifteen years – it's much maltier with less spirit burn. Now an accomplished, silky dram at first with a pleasant build-up of grain and young, under-ripe malt notes (probably from some Glengarioch) which gives it just a sufficient rough edge a standard blend sometimes needs. Even so, a fraction of the 20 per cent malt in this blend is over twenty years old, with small amounts of the now extinct Dunavarty Vatted Malt being used.

Covent Garden 10-year-old
Question. When is a Cutty Sark not a Cutty Sark? Answer: When it's a Covent Garden 10-year-old. This whisky, blended at Campbeltown, is sold exclusively in Cadenhead's cosy little shop in Covent Garden. It is as classical as the operas

performed just yards away with the crispest, cleanest Speysiders you could ever wish for and a playful nip and bite at the throat just to reinforce that this is a blend. Spellbinding whisky that apes Cutty 12 in its mouth-watering qualities. Shades of salt on the nose and finish is a give-away of its origins. An excellent, satisfying blend of unquestionable quality and finesse.

CATTO'S

Along with the James and John Chivas brothers, James Catto was perhaps the best-known whisky merchant in Victorian Aberdeen. The granite city, being both a port and close to the eastern fringes of the Speyside distilling region, became a major commercial whisky centre and when James Catto established his new firm in 1861,

Below
James Catto, a whisky merchant of some renown, in Victorian Aberdeen.

blended Scotch whisky was on the threshold of discovery. Although his enterprise lagged sixty years behind Chivas's, James Catto was canny enough to find a novel way of opening up new markets abroad. As it happened, two of his old chums from his days at Aberdeen Grammar School had founded the White Star and P&O shipping lines. They were more than happy to carry Catto's whiskies to whichever ports they docked around the world. And what was more they could supply it to Scots emigrating to North America and other colonies.

Having established a profitable export trade, James's son Robert set about boosting the home market when he took over the running of the company at the turn of the century. Tragically he was unable to see his plans through as he was killed in France in 1916 while fighting for his country. As James had died in 1908, the executors for the estate sold the business to W. & A. Gilbey who in turn became part of International Distillers and Vintners in 1962. It was with Catto's that the famous former J&B blender Jim Milne learnt his trade but the brand was sold off to Inver House in 1990. Oddly enough, though, when they bought the name they were not given the recipe, and Inver House instead used whiskies brought predominantly from United Distillers in vatted form to recreate the blend.

CATTO'S DELUXE 12-YEAR-OLD
ABOUT THE BLEND

Despite the change in ownership this whisky retains a degree of similarity to how it tasted

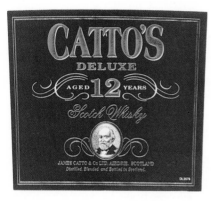

thirty years ago, although it could be closer. The Catto then (no 's', note) had a more Glenlivety grassiness but less age, was a fraction sweeter, cleaner and lighter in texture. But the current Catto's DeLuxe, around 40 per cent (Islay-free) malt-rich, is an older whisky now than then, yet without question both whiskies are to be found in the higher echelons of Scotch blend. Eighteen malts and three grains make up the blend, with North British being the highest-ranking grain, although it is noticeably outweighed by the combined presence of Port Dundas and Cameronbridge. Oban and Ord help add 'pep', and the presence of Aberfeldy, Dalwhinnie and Clynelish also take the whisky away from its old Speyside roots.

NOSE A sensuous light aroma gilded with delicate honeydew melon notes, a clean Speyside citric fruitiness and earthier, oakier tones that offer no more than a hint of a hint. Incredibly complex and fragile.

TASTE Enormous series of mini-explosions on the palate where the almost under-ripe freshness of the clean Speyside malts bombard the taste buds. This enormously busy and delicious start is augmented by a gradual release of richer, oilier notes that slowly coat the mouth and coincide with a rise in the spice level.

FINISH Warming, with a superb chocolate fudge sweetness, topped with a Nice/Malted Milk-biscuity mixture of coconut and malty dough. Superbly clean vanillas and a dash of milk chocolate end this wonderful blend off.

COMMENTS Very few whiskies in the world keep the palate guessing as to what is going to happen next as much as this one does. Every single facet regarding this blend is on the understated, fragile side of things and there is not a dominant or earthy note from start to finish. Even the straw colouring underlines the lightness of this whisky. A genuine cracker of blend for those looking for something rather subtle and rather classy in their lives.

CATTO'S RARE OLD SCOTTISH HIGHLAND WHISKY

A distinctively aromatic blend with citrus-herbal notes often associated with extremely expensive men's perfume. Speyside maltiness has the dominant edge but there is a rich vein of something slightly oily which

gives everything a lift. Heavier, though, than the 12-year-old. To taste, has a silkier, richer and much sweeter feel before the dry, powdery finish. Sweeter than of old and friendlier for all that.

CHIVAS REGAL

To ring anyone connected with Chivas Regal these days, be they in London or Scotland, you will have to dial the number 1801. Which is rather clever, as that is the year Chivas Bros. dates from. Well, sort of. In fact in that year it was a certain William Edward who opened a grocer's and wine merchant's in Aberdeen. It was not until 1836 that James Chivas became a partner and a further twenty-one years elapsed before Chivas Brothers was born. There is an irony, however, that it was not until the Chivas family line ended with the untimely death of Alexander Chivas, aged just 37, (and his wife a few days later) in the early 1890s that the company began to develop its whisky trade to its fullest potential.

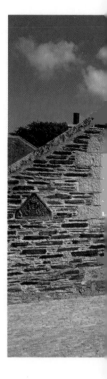

They had based much of their trade on export and within the first decade of the 20th century a brand they called Chivas Regal was finding its way into the North American markets. That included Canada, where the brand brought admiration from Seagram who in 1949 finally bought the company for the sum of £85,000. Seagram then set about acquiring and building a

number of Speyside distilleries, beginning with Strathisla which in recent years and at great cost has been transformed into the spiritual home of Chivas Regal yet which retains its ancient beauty. Seagram has also, often incorrectly, been given the credit for building Scotland's first malt whisky distillery this century with the founding of Glen Keith in 1957. That distinction, in fact, fell to Inverleven nineteen years earlier. That, like

Above
The beautiful
Strathisla
distillery,
spiritual home of
Chivas Regal.

Glen Keith and Seagram's other brand new distilleries, Braes of Glenlivet (now Braeval) and Allt-a-Bhainne, were built simply for the purpose of supplying the malt for a blended whisky famed throughout the world.

ABOUT THE BLEND

Traditionally, a blend of around 40 per cent malt has depended upon the Speyside strength of the Seagram-owned distilleries with Strathisla making up perhaps 4 per cent of the blend. Of late the Strathisla, a powering Speysider, appears to have made a bigger impact, suggesting either it has increased its share slightly or there has been a slight change in the other constituent parts.

NOSE Distinctive apple notes blend in to more exotic fruits, mango even, but the interaction of the grain is often far too austere. The weight of the flat malty tones of Strathisla gives some needed extra lift and body. The old cut-grass crispness has not entirely vanished: in some bottles it is missing, in others it is there but usually to a lesser degree than of yore.

TASTE There can be a deliciously herbal delicacy to the start of this whisky on which soft malts intensify. There is a hint of Strathisla-esque menthol sweetness in the very middle plus some subtle smoky notes.

FINISH When on form the finish is every bit as soft, sweet and alluring as it can sometimes be biting and bitter. At its best the cocoa tang towards the finish is quite superb.

COMMENTS What can you say about a whisky that is regarded, in America in particular, as the final word in Scotch whisky? Well, to be honest, "disappointing" is the one that springs most often to mind. Over the last couple of years this has become one of the most temperamental drams you can find. When in top condition it can be a real sweetie: a touch of class that is as beautifully balanced as you could pray for, with soft Speysiders, a hint of exotic fruit, clean grain and something teasingly smoky and spicy. Too often, though, it is quite ordinary or worse as the nose can be as flat as a witch's chest and to taste proves fiery and unwelcoming with more than a hint of a Strathclyde-esque overindulgence. From the 70s onwards a bottle of Chivas would be found in my student flat and it was a whisky I grew up with and near worshipped. Today, though, it is just too much of a lucky dip to find a bottle that justifies the price. It breaks my heart to say it, and I just hope it is a phase it is going through. When you consider that such great malts as the incredible Longmorn and classy Glen Grant are from the same stable, as is the lovely Century of Malts and two absolute masterpieces, Chivas Oldest and Finest and Royal Salute, and that they are all under the control of a gifted blender, it is all sadly mystifying.

CHIVAS REGAL 18 YEARS OLD

A heavier, sweeter, more floral aroma with a soft raisiny fruitiness and subtle oaky vanilla; fuller and fatter on the mouth than the 12-year-old again, with a more profound German biscuity sweetness, a pulpy fruitiness and lingering spices and oak. A much more substantial whisky than the Chivas 12.

FAMILY BLENDS
CHIVAS BROTHERS OLDEST AND FINEST

ABOUT THE BLEND
The first corked whisky bottle I have ever opened that emitted a real champagne-style pop – and not without good reason! Launched in Amsterdam in February 1998 for Duty Free alone, each bottle will cost around the $130 mark – and worth every cent.

NOSE Breathtaking. Fabulously weighted with no more than a hint of sherry and a sprinkling of nutmeg and allspice. A beguiling aroma with most un-Chivas-like smoke and peat; the oak is present but subdued and the malt offers at once some flighty lightness and depth. The grains are present but only aid the malts. Classic whisky for the most discriminating.

TASTE No shocks: the taste follows on exactly where the nose left off. The sherry is perhaps just a little weightier than the nose might suggest but the spices are incredibly deft and flit around the palate with incredible speed. The malt is pronounced and builds up to something approaching smoky intensity until the grains intervene and soften them down a little. There is a ripe fruitiness, mainly ripe raisins and sultanas with some succulent plums thrown in.

FINISH Beautifully long, smoky and gorgeously structured with the fruitiness hanging on as some oak arrives. It never becomes quite as intense as a fruitcake, but with a slight nuttiness that arrives it certainly heads that way.

COMMENTS This is perhaps the finest new blend I have been introduced to in the last couple of years. Colin Scott is a blender whose forte is working with extremely old stocks and producing a whisky that shows absolutely no signs of wear and tear. Until this the Royal Salute 40-year-old had been his greatest moment, but I think this tops it because, although it doesn't match that whisky's silky beauty, there is a complexity to this whisky that leaves you astonished. This is a very expensive whisky, and with every nose and drop that passes the lips you can see why. Nothing short of a masterpiece.

CHIVAS BROTHERS 1801

Another astonishing, truly captivating blend from Chivas blender Colin Scot. It is helped along the way by being 50 per cent ABV, in a bid to recreate how strengths of whiskies used to be, and with this intensity comes a blissful intermingling of complexity and power. The nose is smoky and salty and this translates on the palate, only with a quite fabulous sweet lushness thrown in and with a superb grainy bite to remind you this is a blend. A quite singular blend of understated magnificence.

CLAN CAMPBELL

The Campbells are one of the great clans of Scotland, whose seat is the imposing Inverarey Castle. It may be strange to relate, but the whisky on sale to visitors to the castle is not this brand from Campbell Distillers, one of the top fifteen

selling Scotch blends in the world. Instead, they have long sold their own brand, called Argyll, named after the Duke of Argyll whose home Inverary Castle is.

The House of Campbell blending company is not quite so ancient. It dates back certainly to 1937 when Forbes Macgregor & Co. changed their name to S. Campbell & Son. But the

House of Campbell came into existence under that title only in 1988 when the company's name was altered again. S. Campbell & Son had made a point from Day 1 of making its mark on the export trade. It purchased Aberlour distillery in 1945 not only to supply its malt for their blends, but also for exchanging whiskies. As a direct result of its strength abroad, S. Campbell & Son was taken over by the giant French drinks company Pernod Ricard in 1974 and the Edradour and Glenallachie distilleries were also subsequently purchased. By 1983 the stronger White Heather brand along with Clan Campbell, developed in the late 1970s, but a slow starter, represented some 5 per cent of the French market. But by 1990 export sales for Clan Campbell had outstripped White Heather and topped an enormous 750,000 cases a year. Today it sits 14th in the league table of most popular Scotches, selling 1.2 million cases a year world wide, nearly 700,000 of them in France alone.

Opposite
The enchanting Inverarey Castle on the banks of Loch Fyne is the ancestral seat of the Campbell clan after whom this blend is named.

ABOUT THE BLEND

Big Speyside influence with, naturally, Aberlour and Glenallachie having a big say. Although there is some 30 per cent malt to this blend, only three or four non Speyside malts are used. One is Bowmore but in very safe amounts to guarantee a delicate smokiness. Strathclyde and Invergordon are the lead grains. The average age of the whisky is around the 5-year mark.

NOSE Lovely traditional blend nose: grainy and lively but with no bite. The malt is secondary but very subtle and teasing. Just a hint of dough and mint.

TASTE Really tasty see-saw between sweet and dry with the grains forming a hardened edge to the solid maltiness. The sweetness wins out for just long enough to make for a delightful middle.

FINISH Medium length with lots of vanilla.

COMMENTS Some people will doubtless find this a little on the austere side. However, this reminds me of some very old-fashioned blends where the grain played a leading role and the malt filling in any gaps. This is of that ilk, but although there is bite there is no choking, burning roughness. The balance is impressive throughout.

FAMILY BLENDS

CLAN CAMPBELL HIGHLANDER AGED 12 YEARS

A stunning nose from the fruity school: greengages and grapes abound and there is a sweet smokiness to add extra depth. A hint of orange peel rounds off a lovely aroma. To taste, there is evidence of sherry, more orange and some drier herbs and spices. The finish remains bristling with spicy notes to the end despite some flatter cocoa notes. The finale sees in a salty, just slightly over-oaky dryness. But this lovely dram is immeasurably better than as recently as four or five years ago when the grain nipped just a little too playfully.

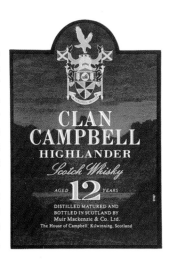

CLAN CAMPBELL LEGENDARY AGED 18 YEARS

A busy, sherried nose with chocolate orange, smoke and fabulous grain softness. Much fatter in the mouth than the other Clan Campbell brands (possibly because of the presence of some Glenugie) with a lingering sweet coffee and peat presence. As is the style with Clan Campbell, the grain has a major say and interacts with the malt to guarantee astonishing complexity in the mouth, especially with a tantalising mixture of vanilla and orange. The finish is clean and quite long. This lip-smacking ultra-complex whisky was launched only in 1997, but on this showing is destined to reach deserved legendary status …for those who can afford it.

Opposite

The ruins of Balvenie castle gave its name to the Balvenie malt which forms part of the Clan MacGregor blend.

CLAN MACGREGOR

It is sometimes interesting to create your own blend by mixing two or more blends together in proportions you feel might work. Word of warning: do not mix Clan Campbell with Clan MacGregor... the results might be explosive! Such was the hatred between these two warring clans that at the turn of the 17th century the Campbells succeeded in having the name MacGregor outlawed, to the extent that anyone bearing the name would be removed of it at pain of death. It was over 150 years before the bloody canon was repealed by Parliament. Today the slaughter of Clan MacGregor continues in America where people tend to spill MacGregor whisky rather than blood: hundreds of thousands of cases of this blend produced by William Grant are consumed there each year.

ABOUT THE BLEND

A young blend with a malt percentage that ranks on the low side. The grain is principally Girvan although some malts of the richness of Tamdhu and Dalmore do help give extra presence to the Balvenie and Kininvie.

NOSE Distinctive grain lead with a whiff of ginger and pepper. The malt is at first sluggish but comes through young and uncomplex.

TASTE Rich and fat in the mouth with a grainy sweetness that justifies the "Smooth and Mellow" on the label. Just a little spiced and honeyed on the middle.

FINISH The grains continue coating the mouth and the spice greets the cream-toffee sweetness that builds up. Lingering and very chewy.

COMMENTS A youngish blend making the best use of sweet grain so that the blend lingers with enormous weight. Wonderfully chewy, moderately complex and very easy to drink: lovely stuff.

FAMILY BLENDS

The Gordon Highlanders

Also from William Grant, this brand, launched in 1994, seems to have been built upon the same Clan McGregor style, with twice the amount of malt although still detached from the Grant family of blends. There is the same sweetness on the nose, but much more spice and now a hint of sherry and other soft, pulpy fruits. The grain is a little more noticeable, however. To taste there is an immediate fattiness that clings to the mouth and the sweetness gathers in intensity. Fabulous grain balance, allowing the malt to offer a barley sugar sweetness and smoke while the grain carries the vanilla. Excellent balance that culminates in a vaguely spicy finale. Another chewy whisky of impressive weight and presence but this always remains on the light side. For me, though, Clan MacGregor offers just a little extra bite and grainy complexity.

THE CLAYMORE

This is one of Scotland's oldest whisky brands, which has passed through a number of hands before today being an important part of the Whyte & Mackay portfolio. Dating back to at least the 1890s, it was originally sold by the famous old Alexander Ferguson company and would therefore have contained whisky from his now lost Tambowie lowland distillery. By 1907 the brand was in the hands of an even bigger company, the Greenlees Brothers, who had an interest in a superior malt, Glendullan on Speyside, and was a sister brand to Grand Old Parr. With an air of inevitability, the company, as MacDonald, Greenlees & Williams, became part of DCL in 1925. The Claymore brand slumbered for a good half a century or so before DCL put mammoth backing into it as the

Below

During The Claymore's chequered history, it was once part of the Greenlees Brothers' portfolio.

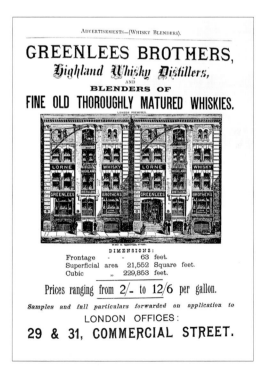

ADVERTISEMENTS—(WHISKY BLENDERS).

GREENLEES BROTHERS,
Highland Whisky Distillers,
AND
BLENDERS OF
FINE OLD THOROUGHLY MATURED WHISKIES.

DIMENSIONS:
Frontage - - 63 feet.
Superficial area 21,552 Square feet.
Cubic „ 229,853 feet.

Prices ranging from 2/- to 12/6 per gallon.

Samples and full particulars forwarded on application to
LONDON OFFICES:
29 & 31, COMMERCIAL STREET.

premier low-price brand for the UK. It was a more a state of DCL's poor blend performance in their home market rather than the quality of the whisky that saw its sales rise to something approaching a million cases by 1977, making it their biggest seller in Britain. However, the brand had to be jettisoned as part of the deal that saw Guinness buy DCL and was sold, with a number of other brands, to Whyte & Mackay. In recent years the quality has been improved beyond recognition by their blender Richard Paterson.

ABOUT THE BLEND

The blend has kept to its traditional Speyside style but this is more noticeable now that some 8-year-old malts have been included in the reworked formula. Still, the percentage of malt remains on the low side, as befitting a low-price product, but the extra age does make the malt shine through a lot more fully.

NOSE Good, solid nose: both firm and soft grains are at play and build a sturdy platform for a mixture of grassy and flatter malts. Just a hint of smoke.

TASTE Fat and lush beyond belief. The sweetness is about as intense as the palate can take, and for some could easily be too sweet. But the tongue appreciates the enormity of the grain-malt battle and continues searching around the mouth for more.

FINISH Long, vaguely smoky and pleasantly sweet with toffee caramel, vanilla, overripe plums and lingering spice.

COMMENTS This is an enormous whisky, far removed from the thin, over-grainy and spirity blend it once was. A lot of work has been carried out to soften everything down. The result is probably the sweetest blend on the market today but the finish is nothing short of dazzling. It goes on for

ever and is multifaceted, with the spice playing a vital role. Tends to suit the female palate in particular. At the bargain-basement price it is sold, no home should be without one.

FAMILY BLENDS

John Barr

Another economy blend from Whyte & Mackay although this time revealing little of the weight and malts that has transformed The Claymore. Certainly better to taste than nose with the unmistakable toffee sweetness of Invergordon grain forming the foundations for the shy, delicately spiced malt. Despite the bitter-ish finale, a blend that offers decent value for money.

CRAWFORD'S

The Crawford brothers were one of a whole batch of blenders who set up shop in Leith during the early 1860s. By 1885 both Archibald and Aikman Crawford had both died, although by then the company was on a sound enough footing to continue. Their most notable brand was Crawford's 3 Star. In 1944 the company was large enough to have attracted the interest of DCL who bought them out. They continued to market the brand until 1986 when Whyte & Mackay acquired the license for marketing and blending rights to a number of their brands including Crawford's 3 and 5 Star.

CRAWFORD'S 3 STAR

This is the big-selling standard brand, in the top dozen or so in the UK, and shows firm grain-vanilla on the nose mingling comfortably with a sweeter malt element. To taste is initially fat and sweet in the mouth, not particularly complex but with a rather attractive chocolate-orange tang towards the finish. The finish itself is deliciously structured with the usual vanilla but with some lingering spices and toffee. Simple but rather pleasant.

CRAWFORD'S 5 STAR
ABOUT THE BLEND
Some 40 malts around the 8-12 year old mark
are married and blended with grains, UDV's in
particular: Port Dundas, Cameron Bridge and
Cambus. This 40 per cent malt blend could soon
be lost to us – make sure you get a bottle before
it is too late.

NOSE A stupendous, honeyed, softly sherried nose with first-class interaction between yielding grain, tropical fruit (pineapples? mangos?), and slightly smoked malt. With the subtlest of spices thrown in for good measure this is about an exotic a nose you are likely to find.

TASTE The early, laid-back softness lulls the taste buds into a false sense of security. The sweetness is more demerara sugar than fruit or honey and then there is a bristling wave of spice to counteract it. The malt is ebullient although, in the Whyte & Mackay style, does not show particularly: it is just there and arrives with tidal wave intensity.

FINISH Long with subtle sherry notes, a tad of licorice, dark fudge and vanilla.

COMMENTS What a delight this blend is. Thick and chewy, there is enormous body to this and a beautiful, clinging maltiness. A quite excellent whisky.

CUTTY SARK

This is a whisky that celebrates an individuality. It is not just the fact that it regales in its unusual although by no means unique title of "Scots" Whisky, as opposed to Scotch. Or that the hand-drawn and lettered label has barely changed in the seventy-five years of the brand's existence; or that the contents are as light in colour as they are in character. Really, it is a mixture of all these things plus, possibly, the peculiarity that the most famous whisky of one of England's most venerable drinking institutions, Berry Bros. & Rudd, can, with rare exceptions, normally only be found outside British shores.

Cutty Sark is about as good an example you will find of the successful invention of a fresh identity. Berry Bros. & Rudd were already a well established concern before they created their new Scotch (or should that be Scots...?). Their address at No. 3 St James's Street was already in the heart of the most desirable quarter of London. And although their business, in one form or another, dated back to the 1730s it was a further 200 years before the whisky was to make its bow.

The sign hanging from the shop shows an old coffee mill, depicting the activity of one Widow Bourne who in 1699 opened a grocer's shop in which coffee was ground. In 1731 the business was taken over by William Pickering. The Berrys were direct descendants of Pickering and in 1810 the Berry name was painted above the shop for

Opposite
Like Ballantine's, Cutty Sark benefitted greatly from the black-market generated by Prohibition in the USA.

the very first time. It was a further century before 'Rudd' was added: Hugh Rudd was a wine expert, from the famous Rudds of Norwich, who became a junior partner at the end of the First World War.

It was Hugh Rudd who had a direct involvement with the creation of Cutty Sark. While lunching with his partners Francis and Walter Berry at No. 3 St James's Street, the conversation swung round to Prohibition in the United States and their own situation with exporting whisky. The date was Tuesday, 23 March 1923 and the "noble" experiment was two months and one week into its fourth year. Before Prohibition only small amounts of whisky had been exported across the Atlantic but the three men, in the company of a fourth – the Scottish artist James McBey – set about creating a new whisky which just might be appreciated by the thirsty citizens of the United States of America. The men had already noted that vast amounts of Canadian whisky were being consumed now that bourbon was almost impossible to find. Canadian whisky was lighter in character than the American's native drink and from the outset it was decided to make a whisky that was caramel free, leaving the lighter, natural colouring of Scotch untainted. Also, the whisky being a blend of predominantly Speyside whisky and grain would guarantee a light flavour character. The whisky made its way into America mainly from the Bahamas, principally through a contact of Francis Berry's, Captain William McCoy. Cutty Sark whisky became, quite literally, an original McCoy.

It may not have been coincidence that the label and name of the whisky designed for these high speed runs was Cutty Sark, the name of a clipper built just a few hundred yards from where the Dumbarton grain distillery was to later be erected. It was a vessel that had set a record time in crossing from England to Australia and after a time serving the Portuguese had just returned back to British shores. The label was designed and personally drawn by McBey. The only change came with the colour. Originally meant to have been creamy-brown to denote age, it came back from the printer vivid yellow, a vision so startling that Berry Bros. & Rudd decided to keep it. With the inevitable demise of Prohibition the whisky was sold into the country legally. In 1961 it reached the heights of being America's most popular Scotch, although it has since been surpassed by others. Today the brand is jointly owned by Berry Bros. & Rudd and the firm responsible for blending it, Robertson & Baxter.

ABOUT THE BLEND

Tamdhu, Glen Rothes and The Macallan are three of the major influences in this Speyside-clean dram with some Invergordon fattening up the predominant North British on the grain.

NOSE Like the Riesling colour of the whisky, the aroma is very light with floral notes. The grain is always present and magnifies the sharp maltiness.

TASTE Brilliant arrival on the palate. Still light in character, the grain now has just a big a part as the malt and they dovetail superbly. Those sharp, grassy Speysiders remain evident and the whole whisky is bolstered by a slightly sweet but unmistakably oily presence that coats the mouth.

CUTTY SARK

BLENDED SCOTS WHISKY

100% Scotch Whiskies from Scotlands best Distilleries

BY APPOINTMENT TO HER MAJESTY THE QUEEN
WINE & SPIRIT MERCHANTS

BERRY BROS & RUDD LTD
ESTABLISHED IN THE XVII CENTURY
3, ST JAMES'S STREET, LONDON
40% vol.   e 700 ml
Product of Scotland

Distilled, Blended and
Bottled in Scotland

FINISH Here just the faintest hint of smoke arrives with the oaky vanilla. Dries and becomes bitter, even, with the faintest thread of chocolate at the very end.

COMMENTS Whenever I encounter this in a bar outside the UK, it is hard to resist, as is any such celebration of the blender's art.

FAMILY BLENDS
CUTTY SARK EMERALD AGED 12 YEARS
Crisp, green malt, mouth-watering grains from the very start on the nose leave you in no doubt that this is a blend and the rich, uncluttered Speyside malt which beautifully intermingles with the grain confirms also that this is a Cutty Sark. Breathtakingly delicate on the palate; a

genuine feast of deft Speyside malts. High quality sweet-dry balance with limited complexity due mainly to a lack of base nose. The finish in particular is delicious with sweet malt fighting it out with the drier oaks. A gentle treat.

CUTTY SARK DISCOVERY AGED 18 YEARS
Much fuller on the nose with soft sherry notes and even a hint of mint and smoke. The malt is quite profound but the grain adds a lovely sharpness, creating almost a 3-D effect. That richness on the nose is magnified many times on the palate. Although toffee sweet, the creaminess extends to the spicy malt and then an explosion of malty tones which range from soft and chewy to momentarily high and fluting. The whole whisky seems to be in stereo with flavours and counter-flavours flitting from one side of the taste buds to the other. A personal favourite.

DEWAR'S WHITE LABEL

This is not only America's best-selling Scotch, but the most expensive whisky brand ever bought. When Guinness and IDV merged, alarm bells in Monopolies Commissions around the world began clanging. To quieten discontent it was agreed that the merged company, named Diageo, would part with one of the old DCL mainstay brands, Dewar's. The battle for Dewar's was conducted in secret although the main players were thought to be two giant independent distilling concerns with big marketing teams but no super league Scotch blends to work on. They were Brown Forman, owners of Jack Daniels, and Bacardi. It was the rum company that won the day by paying £1,150 million, narrowly edging out the Louisville-based family whiskey firm.

For their money Bacardi also got Bombay Sapphire gin and, to the doubtless chagrin of blenders at United Distillers, four distilleries: Aberfeldy (Dewar's first distillery), Craigellachie,

Right
A Dewar's ad.
lays claim to
ancient heritage.

Aultmore (linked with Dewar since 1923) and
Royal Brackla. Few will consider Brackla a loss
but the acquisition of the Aberfeldy and
Craigellachie, where two of Scotland's most
sensational but underrated drams are made, will
be deeply mourned in Edinburgh. The entire
event would have been meat and drink to
wheeler-dealer Tommy Dewar. He had joined his
family's firm in 1881 and was to make an
extraordinary impact. John Dewar & Sons was
originally one of a number of wine and spirit
merchants to be found in Perth. After learning
his trade in the cellars of a relative's wine and
spirit business he opened his own shop at 111
High Street, Perth, in 1846. At first it was single
malts he dealt in but as blends became more
popular he and son John were not averse to
working with them. By the time Tommy joined,
his father had died and he set out travelling
around Britain and the rest of the world,
expanding the company's business by appointing
agents while brother John remained in Scotland
making sure there was enough whisky to keep up
with Tommy's orders. One method was by
building their own distillery, which they did with
Aberfeldy, completed in 1898. The blend that
Tommy put his efforts into was Dewar's White
Label. And he had a lot of fun along the way. He
tried every way possible to get his brand known,
from using pipers to draw attention to it (and the
piper still appears on the label) to making the

first ever commercial: he even built at Waterloo Bridge, on the south side of the Thames, a giant kilted Scotsman raising a dram, the largest electrical advertisement of its day. The success and financial rewards of his larger-than-life marketing were obvious: in 1895 he became just the third person in Britain to own a motor car, a Benz. The first was the Prince of Wales and second was the tea magnate Sir Thomas Lipton. And, like James Buchanan, he also took a keen interest in horse racing and breeding thoroughbreds.

In their later years both Dewars were to find their way into the House of Lords, although not before they had each been to the House of Commons, Tommy a Conservative, John facing from the other side as a Liberal. However, in his younger days as he built the company into one of Scotland's big three, Tommy spent little time in the House and preferred instead to globetrot, even into the White House where President Benjamin Harrison was known to keep Dewar's by the barrel. During 1914 and 1915 there were long consultations between Dewar, Buchanan's, John Walker and Mackie (of White Horse) with a view to an enormous merger. In the event only John Dewar and James Buchanan became partners, calling themselves first Scotch Whisky Brands, then Dewar-Buchanan. In a way it was fitting: Tommy Dewar and Jimmy Buchanan had been similar peas in a pod, both using enormous energy and charisma to build not only

Opposite

Tommy Dewar was among the Whisky Barons of the early 20th century who enjoyed a playboy lifestyle and, like Jimmy Buchanan, took a keen interest in horse racing and breeding. This 'playboy' image was carried through to their advertising campaigns.

their brands but the social acceptability of Scotch whisky and blends in particular. As it happened, Dewar-Buchanan did link up with both Mackie and Walker when DCL took them all over in 1925. With Dewar's effectively back on their own thanks to Bacardi it is hard not to imagine the spirit of Tommy Dewar willing for the brand not just to be Number 1 in the USA, but the world over. But only if achieved with style.

ABOUT THE BLEND

The whisky has undergone a big fundamental character change from the old days. Before the war, and just after, it made a point of stating it was "Of Great Age" although it didn't say what. Certainly it was with much more peat on the nose and palate and the fat sweetness distinctly malty in the local Perthshire style: heathery with a stratum of honey running through it. The grain came through almost as an afterthought. In short, it was quite stunning. Today's blend is younger, lighter and more workmanlike with much less emphasis on the nearby distilleries although Aberfeldy still plays a leading role.

NOSE Unbelievably light compared to how it once was: the soufflé nose among the high quality portfolio blended by UDV. Despite the crisp, clear grain the malt still has a lot to say but in an untaxing and unpeaty way. For maximum character warm a little in the hand which releases the heavier malt notes which are quite toasty.

TASTE Good mouth-feel with impressive bitter-sweet balance. The malt arrives much more early than on the nose and forms a solid base for some honey notes and some lingering smoke and spice. The grain is very even and soft.

FINISH For a light whisky the finish is amazingly long. Vanilla dominates but the honey lingers on and combines beautifully with soft peat.

COMMENTS The nose at first suggests that this whisky might be bland. A splash of water suggests this may not be so; the whisky warmed in the hand confirms it. This is that rarest of breeds: a light whisky that somehow shows just a hint of peat yet is full and complex on the palate. A very popular whisky and deservedly so.

DEW OF BEN NEVIS

Few whisky names date back quite as far as this old brand that is associated with the legendary distiller "Long John" MacDonald. In 1825 he set up his distillery at Fort William within hiking distance of Britain's highest peak, Ben Nevis. In his second decade of enterprise he bottled his single malt and gave it a romantic epithet: Dew of Ben Nevis. The brand lasted well into the 20th century, but in the latter stages of the 19th it was switched from a single malt to a blend.

A curious turn of historical events saw the Long John name heading in separate directions from Dew of Ben Nevis (*see* Long John). In 1981 they were re-united when the Long John

company bought the Ben Nevis Distillery and with it the Dew of Ben Nevis brand. Long John did little with either and it was not until it was purchased by the Japanese distillers Nikka in 1989 that the blend was seriously resurrected, although mainly to satisfy the demands of the 40,000 visitors who inspect the distillery each year. It is a blend deserving a much wider audience.

Opposite
The snowy peak of Ben Nevis – romantic inspiration for the blend, The Dew of Ben Nevis.

ABOUT THE BLEND
Blended by Invergorden. Not yet including much Ben Nevis malt.

DISTILLED AND BOTTLED IN SCOTLAND

Dew of
BEN NEVIS
BLENDED SCOTCH WHISKY

BEN NEVIS DISTILLERY (FORT WILLIAM) LIMITED
PRODUCE OF SCOTLAND
70cl e   40%vol.

NOSE Pretty solid grain presence to start, but softens as it warms in the glass. Beyond that is a core of sweetish malt and very faint smoke.

TASTE Good, sweet arrival on palate; again the firmness of the grain is to show and then sweetens out further towards a malty, although non-taxing, middle.

FINISH The faintest hint of spice and smoke brings some extra life. Very long finish for a blend of this style which remains sweet and vaguely honeyed for quite some while before it becomes quite a dry finish with some echoes of toffee and vanilla.

COMMENT A deliciously firm, steady blend that improves the longer it stays on the palate. This is classic standard blend, stuff of the old school, complete with that reassuring bite on the swallow. Wonderful!

FAMILY BLENDS

DEW OF BEN NEVIS 12-YEAR-OLD

A great aroma to this one: delightfully floral with a hint of mint. There is a lovely heather-honey touch to this one, too. Also just the right amount of smoke to weigh it down. To taste is mouth-filling, slightly viscous at the start, malty and slightly peaty. At the finish the grain finally overcomes the malt but is cushion-soft and some excellent cocoa notes towards the end rounds it off perfectly: about as soft as a blended whisky gets.

DEW OF BEN NEVIS 21-YEAR-OLD

Big and extremely bourbony on the nose with

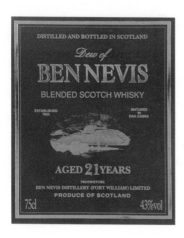

some spearmint and cloves adding to the enormous apple fruitiness. To taste, begins sweet with acacia honey and raisins. Very rich malt and toffee, or maybe toffee apples, and maple syrup arrives towards the middle. The finish becomes more and more spicy as it continues. The oloroso-esque sweetness builds up with a hint of smoke. This flagship blend boasts enormous character throughout; the fruit, sherry and peat combination is irresistible from first to last. Rather bourbony, but classy stuff.

DIMPLE

Known as "Pinch" in its popular North American market, this de luxe blend is an off-shoot of the famous Haig family. The company Haig & Haig was started in 1888 by John Alicius Haig, whose brother Hugh Veitch Haig became a director of the blenders John Haig & Co. "JA" immediately set about selling his famous dimpled bottled whisky to the US. But within ten years the company had gone into liquidation. However, the business was bought by Robertson & Baxter who eventually sold it, in a far healthier state, in 1925 to DCL. They sold the brand alongside the fabulously successful Gold Label and became one of Britain's favourite pre-war tipples.

ABOUT THE BLEND

This is a high malt blend, with grain being in the minority. As is the Haig tradition, Glenkinchie plays a big part with Linkwood following the lead. Some old Clynelish is doubtless responsible for some of the fun at the end while the Teaninich will add a softly smoked maltiness. Of the grains some rare Caledonian and Cambus will add a touch of panache.

NOSE A surprisingly sharp, slightly acidic nose with unwelcome spirit burn. Beyond that there is a flat malt note and little general complexity. All rather disappointing.

TASTE Much softer on the palate with an immediate, although brief, Speyside malty theme. The grain then arrives to thin things out before an enormous wave of very flat, almost nondescript malt arrives. By now things have spiced up a little and the first traces of smoke are making a welcome distraction to the messy, uneven middle.

FINISH At last we are now talking about class. This is nothing short of fabulous, with the peats picking up a heathery buzz and the toffee-vanilla keeping things sweet. Excellent spice also bounces around the palate and then some very dark chocolate arrives to finish things off. Fabulous, although be warned: I have tasted the occasional one or two that are below par.

COMMENTS This is a blend that takes a long time to get going. I have never really come to terms with the nose and the beginning on the palate just doesn't seem to gel in the classic UDV style. But the middle and finish are nothing short of sensational, with the tongue working overtime with the taste buds to keep on top of all that is happening. Best when drunk at full strength and then with a large mouthful. The finish will keep you gripping the edge of your seat for seemingly hours.

DUNHILL

The brand was launched in 1981 as a marketing partnership between Alfred Dunhill and IDV to further the range of Dunhill's exclusive men's accessories. Even so, there are women I know who very much enjoy the whisky! The alliance split in October 1997 when Dunhill linked up with Highland Distilleries with the blending now carried out by Robertson & Baxter. In 1993, to mark their centenary Dunhill came up with the most expensive whisky of all time. They filled 100 casks with a blend of whiskies from distilleries in operation at the time of Dunhill's foundation. The honour of buying one of these exclusive casks cost the customer a cool £43,000. And there were takers, although I believe some of these barrels are still available.

DUNHILL OLD MASTER
ABOUT THE BLEND

Robertson & Baxter have tried to keep as close as possible to the original recipe with North British remaining the main grain. However, they have slightly increased the use of Glen Rothes and Tamdhu among the malts.

> **NOSE** Classic haughty blended character: the grain and malt notes are quite profound and both in equal measure. Vanilla and soft smoke add extra dimension to the flat malty tones.

TASTE Immediate big, silky mouth presence with the grain and malt being inextricably linked. Enormous complexity with some herbal qualities adding to the light grain and heathery-honey malt notes.

FINISH A hint of liquorice and smoke add to the lingering vanilla and spice.

COMMENTS The nose might not be as delicate and Spey-rich as before (indeed, this was for me perhaps the classic Scotch blend on the nose) but the fattening-up of the blend has done it no harm at all on the palate. Remains a brilliant blend but these days for the complexity on the palate alone.

DUNHILL GENTLEMEN'S SPEYSIDE BLEND

A much softer, honeyed, richer blend on the palate than Old Master with deeper bass notes and lots of dark roasted, nutty fudge. When first launched the grain was more easily noticeable and although this is also superb stuff, the Old Master edges it on account of the grain ensuring just a extra degree of bite and complexity.

THE FAMOUS GROUSE

Perth in the mid-19th century must have excelled as the place for whisky shopping. You might have stopped in to try the whiskies of John Dewar. If not quite satisfied, you might have popped across to see Arthur Bell. Equally, you may have started your quest at Matthew Gloag's, a one-time butler who had married into the grocery and wine trade, who set up his own business in 1820. It was William B. Gloag, the son of the founder, who moved into blending whisky

TREASURE FROM SCOTLAND

THE FAMOUS
GROUSE BRAND WHISKY
Matthew Gloag & Son, Perth, Scotland

from single and vatted malts when he took
control during the 1860s. In the 1890s he
adopted the grouse as the firm's motif and called
their top-selling line The Grouse Brand, partly
no doubt to attract those who came to the
Highlands for the good shooting. After a while
customers began to call for the "The Famous
Grouse" and Gloag's duly patented the brand just
so. The moderate success of the brand, and the
undercapitalisation of the Gloag business, in
1970 attracted Highland Distilleries who
successfully set about making it Scotland's
biggest-selling blend. Seizing on the need for a
lighter style blend, they achieved the million case
sales milestone by 1980, thereby having
increased sales tenfold within a decade. Even

today sales of the blend continue to rise. Calls in the bar for a low flier may get you a Grouse, but certainly doesn't represent the brand's remarkable transition from a standard but fondly regarded whisky into Scotland's favourite and the second most in demand within the UK.

ABOUT THE BLEND
The malty base of Glenrothes and lingering sweetness of Tamdhu are evident throughout, with some Macallan adding a bit of extra Speyside depth. The grains, which make up over 65 per cent of the blend, play a crucial role and depend on an intriguing mixture of North British firmness and the reliable softness of old Cambus that has aged at least eight years.

NOSE One of the lightest, most elegant, noses of any blend you are likely to find. Except here the grain seems so confident and clean that it adds an extra richness that seems to go hand in hand with the crisp, equally spotless malts. Green ripe crushed barley is the key aroma by which all else hangs.

TASTE Here the whisky really takes off. Although light and decidedly grainy, this is no slouch on the taste buds. That fresh greenness on the nose is accentuated on the palate: marauding, mouth-watering barley and Speyside notes gang together to make for a fuller, much more deliciously intense mouth-feel than the whisky is often given credit for.

FINISH Really impressive. Quite long for a whisky so light, there are some belated signs of peat smoke and unmistakable oak and toffee apple. Also just a little spice buzz can be felt before the grains take control for the finish.

COMMENTS A lovely blend from the top drawer. This has long been a favourite in Scotland and who can wonder why. Beautifully structured with superb interaction between the subtle malt and the big, fruity grain. In many ways it is a role reversal of the standard blend where the malts have the biggest say. A quite brilliant blend.

THE FAMOUS GROUSE GOLD RESERVE 12-YEAR-OLD

Wonderfully honeyed on the nose with a big malt presence; here the grain is really back to a supporting role. An enticing smokiness on the nose is evident early on the palate but this dies out to allow an apple-fresh fruitiness to take over. As the blend dries so the oak becomes more prominent with vanilla and coffee notes becoming more pronounced. A lovely whisky where the malt plays a greater part than in the standard bottling. Yet, oddly enough, it is the everyday Grouse I prefer.

FAMILY BLENDS
Brig O' Perth
Here's an old friend of mine that I used to drink regularly in Perth during the early 80s but tragically find almost impossible to locate these days. The label, displaying a line drawing of the city's old bridge long before Bell's recent adoption of it as their own emblem, gives the feeling more of a Médoc than Scotch. But the full-bodied, smoky aroma, very distant in character to Gloag's Grouse brands, leaves you in no doubt that this a blend of genuine quality. A honeyed thread on the nose is also found on the palate where an intense 43 per cent ABV smokiness is matched by superb spices and blackberry and redcurrant fruity tones. Like the Dewar's of old this shows great Perthshire character, and although the grain is quite hard at the end it fails to lessen the complexity. A genuinely old-fashioned blend for the connoisseur.

GRAND OLD PARR

Lying in Westminster Abbey are the remains of one Thomas Parr who died in 1635 supposedly in his 153rd year. It is said that even after he turned 100 he was marrying women and fathering children like a lad in his twenties. Very little surprise, then, that that virile specimen of manhood should have been chosen by a whisky company as the name of their top range old blend. Truth to tell, he was not a spirit drinker by accounts, preferring beer and cider: "But then," as UDV blender Gordon Neilson once pointed out to me, "would you have drunk whisky in the early 1600s…?"

The whisky company to launch the brand was the well respected Greenlees Brothers, a wealthy family that entered the whisky trade in 1870. With success not only with Old Parr but with their cheaper Claymore brand, they purchased the Glendullan distillery (malt from which is still used in the Old Parr), in 1919 becoming MacDonald Greenlees & Williams in the process. They dropped the Williams tag (Williams were the first owners of Glendullan) in 1925 and in 1926 became part of DCL. The brand is still owned by DCL's descendants, United Distillers and Vintners, and remains a very bright star in the export constellation.

GRAND OLD PARR AGED 12 YEARS

ABOUT THE BLEND
Big sherry presence is carried on; among others, its lead malt, the complex Cragganmore. Again the Speyside duet of Glendullan and Aultmore are used to lighten things with their Speyside verve. Grain represents only half of this blend and, among that, two lost distilleries are used: Caledonian and the silky Cambus.

NOSE Attractively sherried, a hint of bourbon sweetness, grapey and spicy.

TASTE Very big mouth-feel. From the start there is an intense, moderately oily mixture of peppers, demerara sugar, Java coffee, and very earthy malt. Beautifully complex and roasty.

FINISH Oaky with clean vanilla but a late burnt fudge, sherry and cocoa finale.

COMMENTS A really no-holds-barred, blockbusting whisky that is not for the squeamish. Throughout there is a roasty theme with the sherry lingering throughout but never dampening down the show. The antidote for those who struggle with J&B, Grouse and other light whiskies.

FAMILY BLENDS

OLD PARR SEASONS

This is a conceptual group of blends which at first sight appears a little twee, but on reflection reveals itself as a quite fascinating idea. This is a "Limited edition" blend sold in 50cl bottles, presumably in a bid to help encourage drinkers to collect the entire set. There are four different whiskies: Spring, Summer, Autumn and Winter. Starting with Spring as the lightest, they get heavier in colour and character. Launched in the spring of 1998, just as this book was being completed, this for me is a wonderful way for whisky drinkers to discover the joys of matching different styles of Scotch with matching moods. Clever stuff. And not least because you cannot pick a clear favourite among them: they are all exceptionally fine at representing a high quality blend at the weight they are meant to be and move effortlessly from one gear to the next without a single jolt.

Autumn
Where the Summer shows just a hint of smoke, this depends more on spice to get things moving. There is also a soft graininess that at first suggests lightness then extra fruits arrive offering extra succulent richness. Delicious smoke hangs on the finale.

Spring
The lightest, with a refreshing lemon zestiness on the nose that is well matched by the mouth-watering grassiness on the palate. In the J&B and Cutty 12 school of flavoursome whiskies that is genuinely thirst-quenching and revitalising.

Summer
A much maltier affair. Heavier on nose and palate, there is less Speyside youth and more emphasis on depth. Not quite so complex as

Spring but something out-and-out malt lovers will die for.

Winter

Generous extra sherry but despite the colour and fruit is not perhaps as deep as one might hope. Pity the log fire on the label isn't a peat one as this needs extra smoke and chewyness to scramble over the sherry influence. Rich and resonant nonetheless.

OLD PARR SUPERIOR

Now the sherry really is taking command but is clean and on the nose, at least, obliterates any sign of the grain. The sherry's no less elusive on the taste buds and despite a superb and all too brief bittersweet spice-and-honey effect there is not really the same complexity as the 12-year-old. For those who enjoy super-smooth sherried whiskies, though, this is a must.

Old Parr Tribute

Again, loads of sherry but this time the balance is better with some very old malty elements coming into play plus the sexiest of spicy buzzes. To taste those spices are first to show and display supreme complexity. Dark chocolate and roast coffee notes are also present and flit around with the clean sherry and toffee. There is a late, toasty, vanilla finish. A whisky of evident great age, but like Old Parr himself, seems to cope with the passing years with remarkable ease. By any standards, this is compelling and wonderfully beautiful whisky.

GRANT'S

Here is a rare case of a company who began first as distillers but made their fortune through blended Scotch by hitting the market at exactly the right time. William Grant, as manager of Mortlach distillery in Dufftown, had managed to accrue some £750 in savings in his twenty years there. Hearing that spare distilling equipment was for sale at old Cardhu, he sunk his money into the foundations of the Glenfiddich distillery that took over a year to build but ran for the first time on Christmas Day 1887. With immediate demand for his whisky he built a second distillery five years later which was first named Glen Gordon but quickly rechristened Balvenie. The 1890s was a period when blended whisky had caught the imagination not so much of a country but an empire. They called their finest blend Grant's Standfast in honour of the clan's war-cry: "Stand fast, Craigellachie!" Such was the demand for their whisky that in 1963 they actually built their own grain distillery, a move that proved priceless with the blend now being firmly established in the world's top ten best sellers. And all this achieved with the company remaining firmly within the Grant family, a situation that proudly remains to this day. Indeed, such is the pride of the company's independence that the Standfast tag has now been dropped in favour of Family Reserve, an apposite name since the number of directors and senior management being of the Grant family runs to almost double figures.

WILLIAM GRANT'S FAMILY RESERVE
ABOUT THE BLEND
Of the forty malts the blender can choose from, twenty-five make it into this magnificent blend, including the newcomer Kininvie. Indeed, William Grant malts comprise some 40 per cent of all the malt used with Balvenie and Kininvie sharing 30 per cent equally between them and

Glenfiddich about 10 per cent. This accounts for the clear Speyside theme. But it is perhaps the teaming of smoky malts such as the superb Craigellachie, Ardmore and Glengarioch, on top of the Islays of Laphroaig and Bowmore, that ensures such explosive complexity. Girvan, being owned by Grant's, naturally comprises the vast majority of the grain but Dumbarton toughens it up a little and Strathclyde possibly adds the banana-ry touch. It is little surprise that over recent years the malt level has risen to a very healthy 35 per cent.

NOSE Archetypal blended Scotch: a sound grain base enriched with fluting malty notes, in this case unmistakably Speyside in overall style, with a faintest smoky depth. Look closer and you will notice that there is not a single off-note, every facet of the aroma is clean yet complex and there is a sweetish fruity edge to it, with pears and bananas. Brilliantly, intriguingly and deliciously structured.

TASTE A firm mouth-feel with the banana/vanilla sweetness balancing the sharper malty tones and a more earthy weightiness. Again, very clean yet complex.

FINISH Very long on account of the slight viscous sweetness that clings to the roof of the mouth and which becomes apparent only when all the other complex notes have quietened down

COMMENTS Grant's Family Reserve is a stunner of a whisky, one of the most complex blends the Scotch whisky industry will ever produce. It has the magical balance between excellent Speyside and smoky malt and distinctive grain. The result is a blend that at once massages and pounds the taste buds. With the Original Mackinlay one of my favourite old-fashioned day-to-day blends: a prize whisky no home or self-respecting pub or bar should be without.

FAMILY BLENDS
GRANT'S 100 US PROOF SUPERIOR STRENGTH
With Whyte & Mackay's 105 this is one the two main full-strength blends on the go and the finer of the two. Retaining the banana-ry sweetness, this is a concentrated version of the Family Reserve. However, there is a subtly different flavour profile, with the sweet, oily nature being more profound, as is an oakyness on the finish and the spice that accompanies it. Intense and excellent.

GRANT'S CLASSIC RESERVE 18-YEAR-OLD

An almost alarming outbreak of sherry and bourbon on the nose, suggesting the use of some prize casks and great age. There is marmalade and also a peaty spiciness on the aroma and this is found on the palate too, but not before the sherry, with a ripe grapey fruitiness, has its say. For the finish the spices return amid some buttery malty notes and vanilla on the grain. Great to find a blend of this age which still has enormous life and vitality. Oddly enough, the standard family reserve stills wins for sheer complexity: which gives some idea of the quality of that whisky.

Robbie Dhu 12-Year-Old
(formerly Grant's 12-year-old)

The nose is startlingly fruity with all the trappings of Glenfiddich at one of its better ages. Delicately smoked, this is a mouth-watering dram with fabulous richness. One of the high-lights is the voluptuous mouth-feel which reaches near-perfection: not too dry, not too sweet; oily but not sticky. And the inter-twining of the harder grain edges and the intense malt is as good as any 12-year-old blend gets. Splitting hairs, perhaps the finish is a little on the bitter side but there is quite distinct peatyness to make amends and this really is cracking whisky.

HAIG

The Haig family name is to the early history of Scotch (and even Irish) whisky distilling as the Beams are to bourbon. The Haigs were ubiquitous, with every one of John Haig's five sons striking out on their own paths into the whisky world, some being more successful than others. They had quite a reputation to cling to. In 1655 John's great-great grandfather Robert Haig had been brought to court for carrying out that most foul of misdemeanours: distilling on the Sabbath. It is known that the errant Robert had farmed in Stirlingshire since 1627, so his distilling practices probably dated from very soon after then. The Haigs were principally Lowland distillers. John Haig married into the Stein family and set up the Kilbagie distillery where Robert Stein carried out his first continuous distillation. While John's older sons went their own way, youngest son William stayed behind to run the family distilling business with his father. William had two sons, of which one, John, went on to build in 1824 the most lasting of all the Haig enterprises, Cameronbridge Distillery (*see* Chapter Three). This was one of the six grain distilleries which formed the Distillers Company Limited in 1877. The Haigs still kept the blending side of the business until that, too, was swallowed by DCL in 1919. Among those who had run the company was Captain Douglas Haig, Field Marshal Haig of World War I fame.

Opposite
The tireless efforts of the Haig dynasty within the Scotch whisky industry makes this one of the world's most famous brands – everybody kens John Haig.

166

D'ye Ken
John Haig?
Quality with Age

Original
Haig Bottle

REGD. TRADE MARK

12/6
Per Bottle

13/6
Per Bottle

JOHN HAIG & CO. LTD   *Scotch Whisky Distillers* MARKINCH FIFE
and KINNAIRD HOUSE, PALL MALL EAST S.W.

His name was used by DCL to market the brand – especially against the anti-drink lobby – and it paid dividends. By the 1930s Haig Gold Label was by far the biggest-selling brand in DCL's impressive portfolio although it has lost ground since.

HAIG GOLD LABEL
ABOUT THE BLEND
The Lowlander Glenkinchie is a vital part of the recipe, being used to form a malty base for such whiskies as the mouth-watering Glenlossie which provides succulence and Linkwood some complexity. The malt makes up somewhere between 35 and 40 per cent of the blend.

NOSE Intensely malty and softly honeyed, there is an effortless elegance to this whisky. The grains are also very discreet and allow the most distant of peaty notes to waft through.

TASTE Sweet and initially malt intense with a gradual arrival of vanilla-carrying grain. An almost custardy sweetness battles it out with a sharper green-apple Speyside effect.

FINISH Gentle oaky tones, coffee, toffee and a soft, lingering peat.

COMMENTS This whisky is almost unrecognisable from the firewater that Haig had become some years back. There is a quite beautiful sweetness and confident malt quality, a far cry from what had once made Haig a byword for why people sought solace in single malt. This is wonderfully complex, but all in a very laid back and soft manner.

HANKEY BANNISTER

The name may, like another blend the Baillie Nicol Jarvie, sound whimsical and far-fetched but in fact the brand is titled after a wine and spirit merchant which established itself in the élite West End of London during the middle of the 18th century. They entered into blending during the boom years of the 1890s and were taken over in 1932 by Saccone & Speed, who had also made their fortune serving the forces, firstly as two separate companies working out of Gibraltar. In 1988 Inver House added the brand to their impressive portfolio of blends by buying it from IDV.

ABOUT THE BLEND
Another Islay-free Inver House blend with something around 30 per cent malt profile. The whiskies used are around four and five years old with the whiskies very similar in style to Catto's, except perhaps with more Speyside evidence. Here, though, North British grain is found in equal measure with Cameronbridge and the heavier Port Dundas which both flatten things a little.

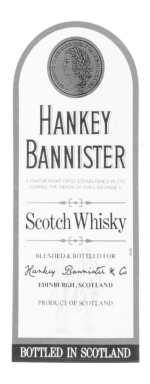

169

NOSE All revolves around a buzzy spiciness which gives an otherwise light aroma extra depth.

TASTE Remarkably clean and toffee sweet. The entire middle consists of old-fashioned cream toffee and subtle malt.

FINISH Medium length and becomes increasingly sweet as more vanilla arrives.

COMMENTS A subtley lightweight dram with excellent toffee carried on the grain, mixing with some enlivening spices.

HIGHLAND QUEEN

The port of Leith near Edinburgh has long been one of the most vital whisky towns of Scotland. It has never been a centre of distillation but before Scotch whisky became an industry it was an important dock for the receiving of wine and spirits from other countries into Scotland. With the bonding facilities that sprung up around it, it was then a natural port from which to "export" whisky first to England – where there were different taxes paid on spirits – and then the rest of the world.

Opposite
The Highland
Queen is named
in honour of
Scotland's ill-
fated monarch,
Mary.

MacDonald & Muir were one of scores if not hundreds of whisky companies working from the old port of Leith, and had their headquarters at various addresses there between 1893 and 1995. Their offices were close to where Mary Stewart, Queen of Scots, landed from France as a teenager in 1561. This blend, created by Roderick MacDonald in his formative year with Alexander

·MARIE· STVART ·REYNE· DESCOSSE·
·VEVFE ·DE· FRANÇOIS· SECOND·
· ROY·DE· FRANCE ·

Muir, was the first his company was sending out onto the market and named it in honour of Leith's connection with the doomed Highland Queen. It was principally on the strength of this brand that the company flourished and became powerful enough to absorb other blending companies and acquire Glenmorangie and Glen Moray distilleries, all within the first two decades of this century.

ABOUT THE BLEND

A standard blend with the malts being at around the 30 to 35 per cent mark. Fifteen 5-year-old malts used in all and two 4-year-old grains, mainly North British with some Strathclyde. Islay takes the back seat with only a small percentage being used. Again Glen Moray plays a vital role and is probably one of the better malts in use. Despite being a Glenmorangie Plc brand, no Glenmorangie is used which partly accounts for why the whisky has no discernible top notes.

NOSE A sumptuous yet unmistakably grainy nose with an enticing "Turkish Delight" sweetness and some clipped, grassy Speyside notes topped with a squeeze of lime. Perhaps a hint of caramel intervenes.

TASTE A momentarily firm then predominantly soft mouth-feel at the start with an early spurt of clean, floury malt and then just a hint of that lime-citrus tang. But the grain kicks in very fast, revealing lots of vanilla and cocoa and swamps all else.

FINISH Medium length and entirely untaxing. The grains hold well and there is some evidence of oak near the finish.

COMMENTS This blend is as clean as a whistle throughout. The Islay contingent hardly makes its presence felt so there is very little weight to keep the graininess in check. That said, this is an exceptionally easy, accessible whisky to get along with and is particularly fine as a thirst-quencher with a little water and ice on an extremely hot day. Not like the Highland Queen I remember from years back, which was a lot fatter and malt-rich on the palate and sweeter all round.

ISLAND PRINCE 15-year-old

Classic half-Scotch/half-bourbon aroma that some better blends at this age achieve; beautifully sweet on the nose but with an excellent smoke and spice bite. Amazingly light on the palate for its age, flitting over the taste buds with a succession of first grainy then malty, creamy notes. A hint of bananas and cream as the oaky vanilla kicks in with simmering smoke. A gentle giant of a whisky from Isle of Arran Distillers.

FAMILY BLEND
Royal Island Finest 21-year-old
Soft oak and a smoke on the breeze are the main
features of an alluringly nutty aroma. To taste, this
whisky is full bodied on the palate with an early
array of oaken malt but sweetens up as the grain
mingles in. Lovely spice and impressive balance but
not quite the complexity of the Island Prince.

ISLAY LEGEND

In years to come this might become known as Islay
Hallmark if a plan to change names goes ahead. In
any case, a blend launched in the early 1980s by
Morrison Bowmore as an outlet for, principally,
their Bowmore Islay whisky. Can be found on the
island and in select European markets.

ABOUT THE BLEND
Something like 50/50 malt and grain, with
Bowmore showing just what it can do.

NOSE Bruising, undisguised Islay peatyness. Salty and oaky, there is
more peat on the nose of this blend than virtually any other.

TASTE Fabulous sweet peat threaded with honey and heather. The
malt also makes its way through and matches perfectly with a clean
grain that does nothing to diminish the Islay style. Although
breathtakingly intense, there is a lightness to the body that does not
quite tally with the style of the whisky.

FINISH Long, sweet chestnut and peat with chewy malt clinging on
as well. Some oaky vanilla drops in at the end.

COMMENTS My two very favourite types of whisky in the world are Islay malt and rye. This truly astonishing blend seems to marry the peaty earthiness with the sweet intensity one finds in rye. A blend not just for Islay-lovers like myself but for those in search of something that keeps the taste buds working overtime. The sweetness is quite remarkable. A magnificent whisky from the top drawer.

ISLAY MIST

This family of blended whiskies represents a style of Scotch normally reserved for malts. In fact, among the many hundreds of blends to be found, this is a genuinely unique range. The whisky, certainly in its younger years, offers unremitting peatyness. These are drams for those who take their whisky very seriously indeed; blends

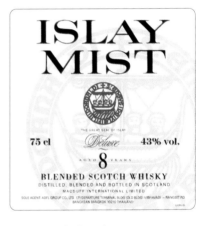

that reach otherwise uncharted depths. The brand itself has been around since 1928 when it was created by the owners of Laphroaig, the Johnsons, to mark the 21st birthday of a local laird. The blend was retained by them and succeeding owners of the distillery until 1991 when it was bought by Macduff International, headed by Stewart Macduff. Although the company does not yet own a distillery, it bought a number of other famous old names, also from Allied Distillers, namely Lauder's and the Grand MacNish.

ISLAY MIST 8 YEAR-OLD

This is the ordinary unaged version, the most common you are likely to find. Classic, young, high-velocity peat whisky with still many of its rougher edges to be smoothed by time in the cask. Having said that, it is a delicious mouthful with enough sweet body to stand a spoon in. Fabulous whisky to keep you going when crossing chill seas by ferry, or when out hill-walking. The grain is entirely overwhelmed by the peat and acts only as a softening buffer on the taste buds.

NOSE The nose is pungent seaweed, iodine peat reek. Sweet malts, a salty tang and a longer grainy note thins things out. Outstanding, especially for Islay lovers.

TASTE Fat, full-bodied peat with a salty, oaky tang and then deep, smoky malt. The grain flits around just lightening the load. Brilliant sweet/dry balance throughout. A real mouthful.

FINISH The peat clings to every nook and cranny in the palate. The grain has vanished save for a vanilla fudge sweetness and hints of coffee.

COMMENTS My love for heavy Islays is well documented, so you must forgive the superlatives concerning this blend, although sometimes it seems hard to actually regard this as one. There is an argument that this is the ultimate blend for the connoisseur: by contrast, it might prove to be the perfect whisky for those who had previously believed they didn't like the stuff.

FAMILY BLENDS
ISLAY MIST MASTER'S AGED 12 YEARS

A very much calmer version where the peat still plays a vital role but a much more honeyed, spicy character balances things out. Certainly on the palate the grain comes through adding some cocoa bitterness and oak while the malt has a dark, fruity depth to add to the peat. A

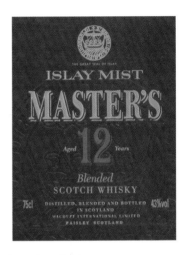

very serious whisky, indeed. And easily the most complex and well structured of the family.

ISLAY MIST PREMIUM AGED 17 YEARS

The storm has now passed and on the nose at least we have a very Perthshire-style heather-honey sweetness with a fine peaty base. To taste, this is initially soft and malt-intense with a strong peaty presence calmed by grassy malt, honeycomb, and then some very soft and light grain. The finish is long with a malty tang and hints of licorice, demerara sugar and spice. A very substantial, beautifully balanced blend.

Grand Macnish

An unusual floral nose with lavender and gorse; a little smoky, too. This smoke continues on the palate, especially for the very long finish. But the middle is fat, intensely malty and earthy. A big, chewable and highly enjoyable whisky but lacking the finesse of Lauder's Finest.

Lauder's

A light, lemon-drop nose of grassy malt and sharp grain is followed on the palate by a sweeter toffee-rich middle and grain-vanilla finish. Totally different in style to Islay Mist and rather ordinary.

Lauder's Finest

A flatter, softer, almost drab nose but to taste is a different story altogether. Just a hint of coffee mingles with intense malt and subtle spice. The vanilla finish becomes dry but a delightfully layered, complex whisky throughout.

J & B

The foundation of this famous old firm is the stuff of BBC costume drama. In 1749 a young Italian, Giacamo Justerini, travelled to England in search of wealth and romance; the object of his desires was a beautiful opera singer, Margherita Bellino; his business partner, George Johnson, was killed by a bolting horse, but not before the Pall Mall-based company had become a pillar of the establishment, complete with royal warrants and the first known newspaper advertisement taken out for Scotch in the London *Morning Post*.

By the time the ad was placed in 1779, Justerini was long back in Italy with his now wife Margherita, although his name lived on in the business. When Alfred Brooks bought the company in 1831, he supplanted Johnson's name with his own so the company became Justerini and Brooks. It is unlikely that Justerini learnt very much about whisky while in England, although through his background in Italy he did know something about distilling, but that was mainly of liqueurs, which he had specially made for him in London. For a century after Brooks's arrival whisky sales were modest, although their whiskies were always considered at the top end of the market, especially their Club brand.

However, it was the launching of the J&B brand in the US following the fall of Prohibition that set the whisky on a path of international

glory. Among the first J&B salesmen was a dashing young British actor-to-be, David Niven, who was also trying to make headway with Ballantine's. The light character of J&B suited the reformed American palate, as Cutty Sark was also discovering. There was a further boost for J&B Rare when Justerini and Brooks amalgamated with W. & A. Gilbey to form International Distillers and Vintners. With the aid of the massive growth of J&B, taking it to the world's second top-selling whisky, IDV became one of the most globally powerful drinks companies. However, in 1998 it merged with Guinness to form Diageo, the most formidable beverage company by a distance, with the distilling arm being called United Distillers and Vintners.

J&B RARE
ABOUT THE BLEND
Although no age statement is given on the label, most of the whiskies found in this blend are around the 8-year mark. The slight upping of the age is probably the reason for a subtle change in style over the last couple of years, with the lead malt Knockando still in its sweet phase. Tamdhu adds fatness, Auchroisk ensures a light Speyside theme, while The Macallan guarantees spice. Of the grains North British plays a crisp, starring role. To underline what a smoke-free whisky this is, of the mere 1 per cent Islay found in the malts, it is part Bowmore, part peat-less Bunnahabhain. Remarkable when you consider that about forty whiskies make up this blend.

NOSE Grassy-clean and citric-fresh, this is an attractive assembly of lighter malts and broad, characterful grain.

TASTE About as mouth-watering as a blend gets: the malt shows subtle spicy qualities and a lip-smacking tang. The grain is also evident, but adds beautifully to the crisp structure. Slightly sweeter than once was, perhaps.

FINISH Lots of grain but this carried a green barley freshness and follows on naturally from the malt.

COMMENTS A fabulously structured whisky that celebrates what can be achieved with a Scotch whisky with little or no peat. One of the most mouth-watering whiskies in the world, but just a little fatter and sweeter than of yore.

FAMILY BLENDS
J&B JET
Easily distinguishable in its all-black bottle and black label with gold and red lettering, the whisky is also easily recognisable in the glass. Few whiskies are quite as sharp as this on the nose with an almost jagged maltiness. Likewise it is immediately sharp and mouth-watering in the grand J&B style but then a sweeter grain note hurries through keeping any hint of smoke at bay. Some oak on the finish. Not quite as sweet as when first launched but can be recognised only as J&B.

J&B RESERVE AGED 15 YEARS
The fattest, maltiest aroma of the J&B family with gooseberries and other fruits on the nose. Soft, dissolves-in-the-mouth maltiness at first, and then that extra-Speyside J&B character emerges. Just a hint of extra smoke on this one but lots of vanilla and soft oak notes towards the finish. The balance is exemplary.

J&B ULTIMA

ABOUT THE BLEND

It would be too easy to dismiss this extraordinary whisky as one designed for the anorak connoisseur, the trainspotters among the world's whisky lovers. No other blend has ever contained so many whiskies from different distilleries – no less than 128 in all. The bottle tells you that it is the life work of J&B's Master Distiller. Actually, that should be past tense: it was Jim Milne,  now managing director of J. & W. Hardie of Antiquary fame, who, working alongside grain specialist Robert McIlroy, created the blend, something he had dreamed of doing for many years and was given the go-ahead to do so to celebrate the 500th anniversary of Scotch whisky in 1994. Most other distillers made a one-off bottling. J&B decided to make theirs a commercial effort. It was moulded in J&B Jet style, making good use of the Benrinnes- and Cardhu-type malts. For the record, every bottle of this whisky contains 116 malts and 12 grains. This, then, is a mouthful of a blend in more ways than one...

NOSE Like damp barley in the maltings: green, refreshing and full of grainy promise. Highly complex with impressive salty, floral-fruity notes but all terribly low-key and beautifully groomed.

TASTE The palate is knocked backwards by a stampede of flavours and whisky styles. As the blend suggests, it as if the entire whisky industry is attacking your taste buds at once. Despite the enormity of the fruity, grassy, mouth-watering flavour profile, it remains light. But the heavier smokier notes do guarantee some flesh.

FINISH Very long and spicy. There is such a plethora of flavours it is hard to exactly pick what is what. Most noticeably towards the finish the malts and grains actually divide and the maltiness is all rather lumpy and flat while the grains offer something just a little crisper.

COMMENTS An amazing whisky, both in concept and execution. The peculiar thing is that, despite all these whiskies on show, it retains that green Speyside character sufficiently for this to be classed in character type among the other J&Bs. Except this is more complex than the others put together.

JOHNNIE WALKER

If there was a time in the world to make your fortune as a humble grocer then it was the mid-19th century. And the place was Scotland. For thirty years John Walker was just one of hundreds if not thousands of grocers building up a respectable clientele which, although not making him rich, guaranteed an income that ensured a relatively comfortable life. His business was founded in Kilmarnock, Ayrshire, in 1820 but it was not until his son Alexander joined the firm in 1856 that he was persuaded that there was life beyond ham, tea and coffee. Whisky had only been sold in the shop for a few years before Alexander's intervention and it had not been given any special status within the store.

The partnership lasted just a year when John died, allowing Alexander free reign to follow his instincts. This was aided just a few years later by the change in law which made the mixing of malt and grain whisky permissible and soon he was working on his own blended mixture. By the time he was joined by his own three sons, Johnnie Walker & Sons were no longer grocers but a Scotch whisky dynasty, a point underlined when the youngest, Alec, took control on his father's death in 1889. The following year James Stevenson came on board to assist Alec and it was he who coined the phrase "Johnnie Walker, born 1820 – still going strong". With those two in control the company expanded further and bought the Cardow, now Cardhu, distillery on Speyside in 1893 and three years later the lowlander Annandale.

In 1908 the name Johnnie Walker was patented and at first they marketed their three existing brands, Old High White Label, Special Red Label and Extra Special Black Label. The cheaper White label fell by the wayside as Red and Black took off globally, helped along the way by the strutting, monocled Johnnie Walker character devised by the cartoonist Tom Browne who a few years earlier had done much work for

BY APPOINTMENT TO HER MAJESTY THE QUEEN, SCOTCH WHISKY DISTILLERS, JOHN WALKER & SONS, LTD.

CLUBHOUSE

Thank you

Johnnie Walker

—there's no better drink than the smooth

round whisky in the square bottle

BORN 1820 — still going strong

the rival blends Teacher's and Roderick Dhu, then a major force on the scene. It is only recently that Johnnie Walker has been completely restyled to lose his jolly if rather smirking facial identity: another example of how whisky companies are embarrassed by links with a bygone age.

However, the whisky has never lost identity, even after the company decided to join forces with DCL in 1925. Johnnie Walker had gone public two years earlier and remained fiercely independent to the end, to the extent of perhaps favouring a merger with Buchanan-Dewar. But in 1925 both Buchanan-Dewar and John Walker & Sons entered the melting pot together, seduced by DCL's enormous capital reserve, although as separate entities. It has been the Johnnie Walker brands that have performed phenomenally, however. In 1997 Johnnie Walker Red was the world's top-selling whisky, moving a staggering 7.9 million cases. Perhaps even more extraordinary is the performance of Johnnie Walker Black, for me the finest blended Scotch money can buy. That sells 3.5 million cases and has closed in to be just 50,000 cases behind the perceived champion of the de luxe blends, Chivas Regal. That means, roughly speaking, that once every 2.77 seconds someone, somewhere in the world is buying a bottle of Johnnie Walker whisky – and that is not including their super premium brands. Perhaps even more remarkable is that in the face of such

Opposite
The famous strutting, monocled dandy devised by the cartoonist Tom Browne for Johnnie Walker.

demand the blenders are capable of hitting the button on quality virtually every time.

JOHNNIE WALKER RED

Recently returned to the UK following an EEC forced exile in 1977. The EEC had clamped down on dual pricing practices which was tied to variable excise rates. DCL decided to banish a number of brands to the export market only, Johnnie Walker Red label among them. Its return has been among the best news for British blend drinkers in recent years.

ABOUT THE BLEND

Has enjoyed something of a revival of late. For a number of years it was just too light with the grains just out of phase with the malts. This has been eradicated by bringing the blend back to a fuller character with both Caol Ila and Talisker combining for smoke and spice, Glendullan to give a solid malt support and Port Dundas grain helping to bind together and flavour the finish.

NOSE Wonderful fusion of light grains with butter cream and peat. The malts rise from the glass as it warms and show surprising honey depth and a hint of apple.

TASTE A full, oily body and a wonderful layer of peat makes this quite a big whisky despite the permanent undercurrent of thin grain. Excellent malt counter-attack.

FINISH Lots of grain on the finish with some delicious vanilla and milk chocolate.

COMMENTS About five years ago this blend just didn't seem to click. But since then it has perked up and become a whisky of outstanding character. Almost unbelievably busy on the palate, the mouth is bombarded with a whisky that is constantly working away and changing shape. Fascinating and absolutely wonderful stuff.

JOHNNIE WALKER BLACK LABEL
ABOUT THE BLEND

Apples from Aberfeldy and Glenlossie, spice from Talisker; malt from Cardhu, lingering peat from Caol Ila, soft smoke from Craigellachie, honey from who knows where. Some thirty-five malts and five grains are found in the recipe of this celebration of Scotch whisky. Certainly individual malts do have an important say. But there are myriad flavours created by a number of fused malts and grains.

NOSE The way the peat and honey hang together and dovetail with the malt, the apples and warming grains, it seems as though the whiskies found in this blend were created just for each other. The secret is that none of these qualities dominate: this is a butterfly whisky with beautiful, graceful notes fluttering around the nose, before landing to be noticed and then moving off again.

TASTE Do not sip this whisky: take by the mouthful, keep it on the palate as long as you can and then swallow slowly. You will be rewarded with an unparalleled exhibition of the blender's work.

Although oily and rich, and working to a fabulous peaty beat, the intensity of the honey and the vividness of the malt and slyness of the spice combine to make this nothing but an experience of unqualified bliss.

FINISH A never-ending finish. The moderate, honeyed sweetness continues; this has now panned out into a raisin, sherry fruitiness and the grains add a lilting, satin-like feel. Dark chocolate and boiled cherries of the finish wrap up an odyssey in liquid gold.

COMMENTS Each day I have some 6,000 whiskies to choose from for a social dram if I want one. And at least once a week I will sample a Black Label. While the single malt revolution continues unabated, it is a shame that whisky lovers do not use this as a yardstick. They will find that very few malts can match this for complexity: perhaps only Ardbeg and Springbank. But even they are left reeling by the all-round charisma that this whisky displays. This is the Savoy, the Everest of de luxe whiskies: there is not a blender outside UDV who would not give their right arm – and even their left one – for the recipe of this supreme whisky. The trouble is, even if they had it, they would then struggle to find the stock. It represents probably the best value for money for any whisky in the world. And despite all the other high performance Johnnie Walker brands to be found around the world, there is still nothing that can quite match this.

JOHNNIE WALKER GOLD LABEL
ABOUT THE BLEND
The idea was to create a whisky lighter than Johnnie Walker Black but accentuating the honeyed theme. To do this, Clynelish has been brought in to play a starring role with Royal Lochnagar not far behind. Talisker guarantees the base and the incomparable grain from Cambus forms the soft bedding.

NOSE Beautifully honeyed but with none of the weighty peat and fruit of the Johnnie Walker Black. The grain is more evident, but offers a superb, entirely uncluttered and focused dimension. A very easy nose to understand.

TASTE Much spicier and sweeter arrival on the palate. Also barley sugar sweetness combines with a malty tartness and then some flatter malt notes of possibly some ancient Speysider.

FINISH The finish is long with renewed spice and a resurgence of honey and vanilla. Some late oily notes bring a slight bourbon-oakyness and some corn-meal malt-chewiness.

COMMENTS One of the most honeyed of all Scotland's blends, this is a rather dapper blend with good malt complexity and some impressive use of grain. Despite being outwardly light and peat-free, still pretty full bodied.

JOHNNIE WALKER BLUE LABEL
ABOUT THE BLEND
It is unusual for a blend to lead on Islay, but here Caol Ila plays a pivotal role and is ably backed by the complex maltiness of Royal Lochnagar and ripe fruitiness of Mortlach. Even a dash of 1923 whisky from the long-lost lowlander Auchtertool is added.

NOSE Deep, but well-aged peat, a splash of sherry, thick malt and some clean grain helping to thin the intensity down a little.

TASTE Lusciously sweet and massively intense. Big fruit kick with a whole basketful of mature, succulent fruits including over-ripe fig, plums, apples and sultanas.

FINISH Big chocolate-mousse follow-through; now there is some lasting malt, there is more of a very old Dundee Cake with just a sprinkling of almonds for good measure.

COMMENTS When this was first launched I thought this was one of the biggest disappointments I had experienced. The grains seemed to be having just a little too much say and there was little or no balance to speak of. With each subsequent bottling the blend tends to get more heavy and fruity. It is similar in style to Johnnie Walker Black except it boasts none of the honey.

FAMILY BLENDS
Johnnie Walker Premier
Sherry and smoke hold the whip hand on the nose although there is even a hint of very old cognac. Lots of oak there, too, and plenty of salty oak and sherry towards the solid, sweet finish. Again, a different shape to any other Johnnie Walker whisky and the big salty, malty tang is absolutely brilliant. Perhaps on a par with Johnnie Walker Blue, although still not as integrated as JW Black.

Johnnie Walker Swing
The aroma is surprisingly vapourish, with a grainy

alcohol bite on the nose. This light-with-grassy-Speyside theme gives no warning of the enormous attack on the palate. Enormous spice kick and then big toffee apple sweetness. A different breed to the other Walker blends and not quite so well controlled. Having said that, it's one hell of a dram.

LANGS

Two bothers, Alexander and Gavin Lang, set out in the whisky trade at that most exciting time of the mid-Victorian period. It was 1861 and merchants had just been given the go-ahead to mix malt whisky with grain, so the timing of their venture could not have been better. They met with immediate success and in 1876 were financially sound enough to buy the beautiful Burnfoot distillery. They immediately re-named it Glengoyne, the whisky from which remains at the heart of their blends today.

It was not until just after the company celebrated its centenary that Lang Bros. were acquired by the famous old blenders and distillers Robertson & Baxter who still own the company and distillery today, although they in turn are part of Highland Distilleries.

About the blend
This has a big malt content, something approaching the 40 per cent mark with Glengoyne playing the lead part in shaping its big, clean-malt style.

NOSE One of the fruitiest you will find: diced green apple, kumquats and grapes. There is a greeny grassiness that is also beyond the malt and seems to stretch into the grain. Brilliant.

TASTE Drier and sharper than the nose suggests, with a very firm, mouth-watering grain presence. The malt remains clean and precise with a slight toffee apple note.

FINISH Medium length, more toffee, a pleasant light spiciness and some lingering vanillas.

COMMENTS This is about as neat and tidy a blend you are likely to discover. The nose is one of the best with untold fruit riches but, although that fruitiness doesn't quite pan out on the palate, everything is mouth-wateringly spick-and-span with just the right amount of malt/grain interaction. Really first-class blending.

LANGS SELECT AGED 12 YEARS
Nothing like so busy or invigorating as the Supreme on the nose with more sherry evident.

On the palate the trademark cleanness is evident throughout, although towards the middle it picks up a cream-toffee-and-nut chewiness. Much more sober than the Supreme and for me not quite so interesting, although the build-up of spice at the death (with a hint of celery!) is highly attractive.

FAMILY BLENDS
Auld Lang Syne

A blend brought out to celebrate the New Year with a play on the word "Langs". As a blend it is pretty standard fare with nothing like the all-round richness or unerring quality of the Langs Supreme; it has good early grain bite but then loses its way with a too sweet, direction-less middle and finish. Its one real claim to fame was that when you open the carton it should play "Auld Lang Syne". However, a few people were bemused to find that the wrong device had been installed and instead of receiving a rendition of the Robbie Burns classic, they heard instead "Home, Home on the Range". If anyone has one, please let me know.

THE LOCH FYNE

Until 1993 Richard Joynson and his wife Lyndsay ran a salmon hatchery. Then they bought a shop in the quaint and beautiful little village of Inveraray, on the west coast of Scotland, whose skyline is dominated by the Inveraray Castle, and have since become among Scotland's foremost whisky enthusiasts. They turned their shop into something approaching a sanctuary to whisky lovers, selling all they could find on the subject, beginning a

whisky newsletter and even introducing their own blend in 1996. For small independent whisky outlets to launch a single malt is nothing unusual. For them to launch a blend is something to be celebrated. While Loch Fyne whisky is sold in a few Argyll bars the vast majority is sold in the excellent Loch Fyne whisky shop. Fortunately for those unable to make it there, their business is also a mail order one.

Opposite
Loch Fyne –
inspiration for a
new blend from
Inverarey.

ABOUT THE BLEND
Blended by Ronnie Martin, producer of the Inverarity brand, this is a lot more impressive than you might expect from a single outlet producer. There are in excess of twenty malts used, very high for a low-case sales product, and three grains. The top dressing is supplied by some top-rate 14-year-old Aultmore, although the usual ages of the whisky used is around the 6-year mark.

NOSE Very busy and well weighted. There is no shortage of smoky, peaty notes to let you know there is malt about while the grain is light and lively. Certainly characterful with some intriguing spiciness.

TASTE The grain travels faster to the taste buds than the malt and offers a hard, grainy start. But that smoke is not far behind to soften and sweeten things a little. Like the nose, the middle proves very busy and bustling with peat and spices making the taste buds hop around a little. There is also a very impressive wave of flighty Speysiders to bulk up the malt when it arrives.

FINISH A big vanilla kick as the oak battles it out with the peat and some lingering caramel. Very long with some sweetish toffee-almond notes before drying.

COMMENTS No shrinking violet this, and tends towards the heavy side of blends. Not for J&B drinkers, but proof that decent use of peat can give a whisky enormous character and lift. Good balance throughout. Highly drinkable.

LOCH RANZA

On 25 July 1998 the spirit of the Isle of Arran Distillery came of age. The distillery, fabulously situated in a natural amphitheatre at Loch Ranza, bounded on three sides by mountains and just a mile from the sea, began distilling for the very first time on 29 June 1995. The spirit was filled into cask on the following July 25th. It is on the third birthday of a spirit being barrelled that it becomes Scotch. And so it was that on that day in July 1998 that it became available for blending for the first time.

To get the distillery built in the first place, the founding father, former Seagram Managing Director Harold Currie, set out on an ambitious programme to sell bonds in return for hard cash.

The plan worked: investors will be receiving mature whisky at regular intervals. But one way to bring in extra revenue while the whisky designate matured in the casks was to turn the distillery into a tourist attraction. This they have successfully achieved and being the only distillery on the island visitors have arrived in their thousands. Unable to sell them their own single malt whisky they linked up with Invergordon Distillers to produce a range of blends across the price spectrum. And as from July 1998 the plan has been to introduce their own Isle of Arran malt into first the non-aged blends and then those with age statements. For that reason Loch Ranza became the first brand ever to include whisky from Scotland's most ruggedly beautiful and spectacular isle.

ABOUT THE BLEND
Produced by Invergordon initially as a minimum 5-year-old blend, but such is the high quality of Isle of Arran whisky that it was immediatly added to Loch Ranza. In the mean time the twenty malts include Tamnavulin and Auchroist; the grain is predominantly Invergordon but there is even some Cambus.

NOSE Malty (although not as grassy as the early days) and confident and against the yielding grain. Very soft hint of smoke and the caramel sweetness of Invergordon grain.

TASTE Sumptuously rich start with the malt offering lots of toffee fudge with a delicious buttery silkiness. Excellent weight and, although complex, not overly so; nevertheless, the class is indisputable.

FINISH Perhaps the high spot of the whole whisky. Amazingly long with tons of malt and caramel grain which is as gentle and sensual as you could pray for.

COMMENTS I have a soft spot for this whisky as I did help choose it for them. But I must say that for a young blend this is balmy stuff: chewy, malty but with that clinging hint of sweetness that balances with the late oaky finale. Not as spicy as it once was, but still a belter.

FAMILY BLENDS
Glen Rosa
Much younger on the nose and palate with the grain dominating throughout. Some very clean malt very early on and towards the finale but overall not a patch on Loch Ranza.

LONG JOHN

This blend is now part of the Allied Domecq portfolio but took a complicated route to get there. The Long John referred to is the legendary Highlander who founded Ben Nevis distillery (*see* Dew of Ben Nevis) but the brand name was bought in 1911 by the London wine and spirit merchants W. H. Chaplin. They, in turn, were bought in 1936 by Seagar Evans, the ancient gin distillers. They had already built the Strathclyde grain distillery in Glasgow mainly for gin but with one eye open for any possible advance into

whisky and with the Long John brand they now had the chance. They immediately purchased the now sadly lost Glenugie distillery at Peterhead for malt supplies and then, in the late 1950s, built Tormore and Kinclaith within the compact Strathclyde complex. Seagar Evans became part of Whitbread, and in 1981 they bought the Ben Nevis distillery where the name and brand had started. The association was short-lived as Nikka bought the distillery in 1989.

Above

The Tormore distillery on Speyside was built by Seagar Evans in the late 1950s to produce grains for the Long John brand.

ABOUT THE BLEND

Laphroaig leads the way for the 48 malts used with Highland Park also a key figure, though

Allied's own Orkney malt, Scapa, does not get a look in. Strathclyde keeps its traditional place as the senior grain though three others are used to help balance things out.

NOSE A sturdy, voluptuously rounded nose; a tantalising mixture of sweet honey, gentle peat reek, slightly green apple and crunchy-crisp grain. Superb.

TASTE Sultana-fruit sweetness and moderate malt. Nothing like so well structured as the nose.

FINISH Thin, short, with rather rough, uncultivated grain and a metallic imperviousness that guarantees a not altogether desirable finale. For me, not enjoyable at all and leaves you gasping for a Teacher's.

COMMENTS It is a shame that the taste doesn't come even close to living up to the nose. In particular the finish is pretty lacking and there is too much evidence of Strathclyde grain to be healthy. Even the late malt tones are extremely hard and unyielding. That said, this is still about 100 times better than the days of Long John and Whitbread when a glass of this would come close to putting you off whisky for life. Since under the wing of Allied, Long John has improved beyond recognition. But still not enough.

MacLeod's Isle of Skye

A small but enterprising and highly respected company based at Broxburn near Edinburgh, just around the corner from Glenmorangie, it can date itself back to the last century when this brand was created on the Isle of Skye by Ian MacLeod. The present owner is Peter Russell, a whisky-broking company that purchased MacLeod in 1963. Since then they displayed commendable allegiance to the spirit of the brand by retaining its peaty island style. They have also begun blending and bottling privately, notably for Sainsbury's and Praba na Linne, owners of Te Bheag.

MacLeod's Isle of Skye Blended Scotch

Less smoky on the nose and more grain dominant. To taste is equally as lush as the 8-year-old but rather too sweet and consequently allows limited flavour development. Excellent grain follow-through and dries out rather impressively. As enjoyable as it is, not as inspirational as the masterful 8-year-old. Confusingly, on the back label refers to the whisky being called Isle of Skye Superior Blended, which it is not called on the front label.

MacLeod's Isle of Skye Aged 8 Years

Above

The mysterious mountain ranges of the Isle of Skye form a dramatic backdrop to the incomparable Talisker distillery.

ABOUT THE BLEND

There is a healthy 40 per cent malt quotient in this blend with Lagavulin offering the Islay, whose enormity actually helps dampen down the phenolic spiciness of the Skye single malt Talisker. These two are by far the most important whiskies to the blend with North British grain forming an impressive frame.

NOSE Stunningly evocative. Deep peaty tones waft from the glass, like the reek from a crofter's lum. But there is a lot more beyond: the grains intermingle deliciously with oaky, vanilla notes and something malty and even slightly honeyed. The stuff of dreams.

TASTE Sweet at first, and remarkably viscous. This seems to be the peat hanging around and there is intense barley sugar and spice. Massively flavoured.

FINISH This creaminess continues for what seems hours. Remains sweet, spicy and chewy and at the end faintly nutty. The oak returns at the end.

COMMENTS A year or two back, I was playing about in a lab ·and mixing a blend for the fun of it, having just worked on a very light one for the North American market. I wanted to make something that you could chew until your jaw dropped off. I made it (and still have the recipe) and it put me in mind of a certain blend. This was it. This is also a close relation to the superb Peaty Creag from the bespoke wine merchants, Tanners, and both these smoky 8-year-olds are, to me, drams that can keep you entertained for hours on end. This is knife-and-fork stuff and brilliantly structured.

MITCHELL'S 12-YEAR-OLD

Opposite

Springbank, a byword among connoisseurs, is one of only two distilleries to survive in the Campbeltown area though the older distillery, Glen Scotia, has been silent for some years now.

This is the blend produced by the incomparable Springbank Distillery in Campbeltown. A little over a century ago some twenty-two distilleries were operating from the small town at the foot of the Kintyre Peninsula, making Campbeltown the then whisky capital of the world. Today only two survive, Springbank and Glen Scotia, although the latter has been silent for a few years now. Springbank has since become a byword among some connoisseurs, myself included, for the finest malt whisky mainland Scotland has to offer. Only small amounts are made of it each year and it is some time since Springbank has been a filling whisky for Scotland's major blenders, although they have recently filled for Burn Stewart and Arran Distillers. Mitchell's 12-year-old and Campbeltown Loch are Springbank blends and are therefore the only blended whiskies to be guaranteed to include Springbank's extraordinary, salt-tangy complex whisky.

Springbank is unique in being the only distillery in Scotland to floor malt all the barley it needs for its entire annual production. And a further distinction is that since it was founded, legally, by the Mitchell family in 1828 it has

remained in the same family hands; and it was from this family that this 12-year-old blend takes its name. The current owner, Hedley Wright, is the great-great-grandson of an Archibald Mitchell who set up an illegal still on the site of Springbank. And although he has proved himself a fine blender with his quite stunning Putachieside for his Cadenhead subsidiary, this blend was put together by distillery manager Frank McHardy who for many years was responsible for the Bushmills blends across the Irish Sea.

ABOUT THE BLEND

Launched in 1997 and made to a high-specification 60 per cent malt / 40 per cent grain recipe. The predominant malt is Springbank, which shows in the character throughout, especially at times when sherry cask has been used. The entire grain used is Invergordon, which perhaps explains why the Springbank has such a clear run. The other malt is made from a vatting of Springbank, Speysiders, including The Glenlivet, and a tiny fraction of Islay.

NOSE Unmistakable salty Springbank springs from the glass with its usual plethora of aromas, but, unlike the single malt, has been dampened down a little by a slightly bourbony grain. Just a slight hint of sulphur is evident but this is kept at bay by a lemon-lime fruitiness and freshly-mown grass.

TASTE Enormously fruity, with a build-up of oily sweetness. Very big mouth-feel with enormous malt presence. The tongue is constantly searching the roof of the mouth to discover what oaky-salty tones will be coming next.

FINISH Oaky with some grainy residue. Very long and enormously satisfying.

COMMENTS Nothing short of magnificent whisky. An absolute must for Springbank fans, of which there are thousands. It is the Springbank that dominates but, taking the nature of that idiosyncratic beast into account, this is hardly surprising.

OLD SMUGGLER

A young, exceptionally light blend from Allied Domecq with enormous grain character on the nose. The grains are also first to show when on the taste buds, but are supremely soft and act as a harmonic fanfare to the malt that arrives in clean Speyside style followed by a caramel sweetness. The finish is a bit grainy and dry by comparison but makes for a really tasty although simplistic blend for all that. The stuff on the back label telling you that the taste of this whisky has been about since 1835 is one of the worst pieces of rubbish written on a whisky bottle. There was no such thing as blended whisky then. The stuff smugglers dealt in was a million miles from this whisky. Enjoy it nonetheless.

THE ORIGINAL MACKINLAY

One of the finest names to emanate from the Leith school of blending. The founder Charles Mackinlay began as a wine merchant in 1815 and, like others in that vital port, began supplying malt whisky as well. The Mackinlay name soon became one of the most distinguished in whisky circles, as did the quality of their whisky. One reason was the strong family bond that saw the company's reins being handed from father to son through five generations until Donald Mackinlay's retirement in 1992. Each Mackinlay was regarded a blender in his own

right and although Andrew Usher appeared to have been the first to master the delicate blending of malt with grain whisky, Charles's son James was not very far behind. James was also instrumental in the building of the now lost Glen Mhor distillery in Inverness and the Mackinlay family also took an interest in another Inverness distillery, Glen Albyn. The company lost independence in 1961when it became part of Scottish and Newcastle breweries and is now Whyte & Mackay's Invergordon arm's flagship brand with the blending duties having been passed to Norman Mathison.

ABOUT THE BLEND

A quite hefty 35 per cent malt for an outwardly lightish blend. Of the twenty-seven whiskies going to make up this trusty old classic there are six grains, an unusually high number in this day and age. Tamnavulin guarantees a Speyside-ish, full malt texture. Of the grains, the softness of the Invergordon harmonises beautifully with the more vivid North British. Significantly, not a single peated Islay is found in the recipe but the smoky, criminally under-rated Ardmore is there to give subtle weight.

NOSE A graceful, complex bittersweet aroma with a rather beautiful mixture of some fulsome malts and something a little younger. Despite some evidence of a little ginger and the merest dash of smoke, the grain lifts the style and ensures a pleasing lightness. A very satisfying aroma: a classic light to medium bodied blend.

TASTE The nose is complex and so, too, is the taste. The grains play a starring role: although never harsh they are at times forceful and help intensify the very clean, grassy malt which forms the backbone of this blend and do nothing to dilute the excellent rich, sweet and vaguely viscous texture. A few citrus notes add a delicate fruitiness and hints of cocoa actually make it into the middle. There is a stylish bite as you swallow, something I always like to find on this style of blend.

FINISH The vanilla-cocoa theme continues with a delightful spice-warming crescendo wrapping up an highly impressive dram.

COMMENTS For many years during the late 1970s to early and mid-1980s this was my usual blend: a bottle or three would always be found at home although the other two dozen different ones would change. In style it falls somewhere between J&B and Teacher's. The grains are softer in character than they were a decade or two back and I think I prefer the old recipe, whatever that was, which was blended under the guidance of Donald Mackinlay. I feared the worst when the blend was taken over: not because of lack of faith in Invergordon, but for a fear of the recipe being altered slightly to encompass their own favoured grain and malts. The pill has been a pleasant one to swallow: there are subtle differences but in essence the Original Mackinlay style has been preserved. Perhaps it is slightly fatter than some might remember, and a little sweeter. But even on a blind tasting I found this a far above average blend, the pick of the Invergordon stable and a tribute to Norman Mathison. Still remains one of the favourite blended whiskies to this day.

FAMILY BLENDS
MACKINLAY'S 12 YEARS OLD
Lovely nose, similar to freshly ground malt. Hint of sherry and boiled, unsugared cherries. Firm arrival on the palate with some firm grain complementing the sweet-ish malt that becomes increasingly spicy. Excellent balance throughout. A little gem.

MACKINLAY'S 21 YEARS OLD
Much more sherry, fruit and oak on the aroma. If anything perhaps a shade too oaky although there is an attractive bourbon-esque sweetness. Initially dry with big oak involvement but this settles down as some sherry and oilier malt tones battle through with some sweet grain and spice. Enjoyable, but for me not a patch on the sublime standard brand.

PASSPORT

*Opposite
The speyside distillery of Glen Keith is a relatively recent operation having been converted from a meal-mill in 1958 to its present function.*

This blend was developed by legendary Seagram blender Jimmy Lang in the 1960s to suit the company's Speyside malts and appeal to those preferring a light and crisp style of whisky. Seagram's still market it for export and duty free alone, where it has enjoyed deserved success lying 10th in the top-selling Scotch brands, shifting two million cases each year.

ABOUT THE BLEND
Seagram own some great Speyside distilleries

including Longmorn, Glen Grant and the greatly under appreciated Braeval. In fact all Seagram's Scottish distilleries are located in Speyside and this is amply demonstrated in this blend.

NOSE Just a little a grainy to start with some soft vanillas breezing through. The malts take a little time to reveal themselves, but when they do they are unmistakably Speyside in style. Very light and simple.

TASTE Excellent early grain arrival linking with some high Speyside notes. Grassy, but someone has attacked the blend with a lawnmower because this is not as grassy as of old. Some very flat and even chewy malty notes hit the middle and there is the most subtle hint of smoke (although not peat).

FINISH Dry and malty although a little raisiny with some flaked chocolate notes.

COMMENTS This whisky is not quite as grassy and mouth-watering as it once was. The malts seem a whole degree flatter than a few years back when Passport was one of the most strikingly mouth-watering and moreish blends around. However, once you get used to its new subdued style this remains a highly delicious blend of the understated, complex school and when on song by far and away the best in the Seagram standard portfolio.

ROB ROY

The brand, celebrating legendary outlaw Rob Roy Macgregor, dates all the way back to 1913. It was revived by Morrison Bowmore, although it can be criminally hard to find in Britain, with the exception of on Islay. Ironically, it sells far better in South America and Asia where few people will have any idea of who Rob Roy was.

ABOUT THE BLEND
Enormously high malt content at 60 per cent with the blender using all three of the company's malts: Bowmore, Glengarioch and Auchentoshan.

NOSE Sweet with a hint of lavender and understated peat. A spicy nose prickle also shows some of the lighter grains. There is an oily saltiness too, similar to a green olive.

TASTE Rich-textured and oily. Clings sweetly to the mouth with a delicious, amazingly intense maltiness. There is also something fruity in there, but almost impossible to pinpoint what, so thick is the mouthful. Certainly the malt is almost chewable and lets in some toffee, vanilla, peat and even the odd grain of crushed black pepper.

FINISH Dry with lots of vanilla and distant echoes of peat and caramel.

COMMENTS Quite a profound whisky with enormous depth. The grain seems to keep at arm's length, allowing the malt to thrive. A delightful whisky to enjoy from time to time and one that has never let me down over the years.

ROYAL HOUSEHOLD

It is a shame this whisky can be found only in Japan these days as it carries a lovely piece of Scottish whisky history. Just after the end of the First World War blenders were invited to bid to produce a brand of whisky that would be used by the Royal Household. The blend selected was one submitted by James Buchanan. It was not a brand-new recipe that was used to win the contract, but a tried and tested one for an obscure blend that was popular in certain, often remote, parts of Scotland. One of those outposts was the Rodel Hotel, on the distant Isle of Harris in the Outer Hebrides. However, Buchanan promised to continue supplying the blend to them as well as the Royal Household, a tradition that continued for many years.

Today, sadly, the whisky can be found neither in the royal homes of England and Scotland nor on the Rodel Hotel on Harris. That hotel has been closed some years now, although it is still owned by Donny MacDonald, grandson of Jock McCallun who managed to secure the continued delivery of what was once one of Britain's most exclusive brands. The Rodel bar remains open and Donny tells me with some sadness that he is often asked for Royal Household, only to disappoint his customers. His dual wish is to reopen the hotel and for the United Distillers Vintners to find it in their hearts to send him a few cases of it each year. In the mean time, to taste this blend you must journey to another set of islands: those that make up Japan.

ABOUT THE BLEND

As is the tradition with Buchanan brands, the heather-honeyed classic distillery of the Highlands, Dalwhinnie, is at the very heart of the blend. Some Talisker helps spice-up the blend and the rich-textured Glendullen ensures a

216

big Speyside feel. Perhaps, though, it is the near 50/50 balance between malt and grain that helps the whisky feel so confident and big on the palate.

NOSE A big burst of Speyside floral grassiness plus a touch of peat, simmering black peppers and clean grain. An extremely crisp nose.

TASTE Launches a big Speyside malty theme on the palate with a lovely array of sharp, fruity notes and delicate, slightly brittle grain. All this is cleverly interwoven.

FINISH Very light with the grain bringing in lots of vanilla and a hint of caramel.

COMMENTS A beautiful, sophisticated blend. Perhaps not quite as mouth-watering and complex as it was four or five years ago but a brilliant whisky all the same.

ROYAL SALUTE

Produced by Seagram in 1953 to commemorate the coronation of Queen Elizabeth II. During the early 1990s there was also a 40-year-old version, one of the finest, most complex, aged blends I have ever encountered, with a background sweetness of Turkish Delight. Sadly there were insufficient stocks to keep that brand alive.

ROYAL SALUTE 21 YEAR-OLD

NOSE The nose of a whisky doesn't come more wrapped in silk than this. Yet there is big character there that means it doesn't give a one-dimensional sweetness. Very soft sherry combines delightfully with salty, oaky notes. A stunning nose, magnificently balanced.

TASTE A lush, spongy maltiness with peppery sherry notes with a slightly salted sunflower seed nuttiness and soft oils. A rose-petal, Turkish delight sweetness hides behind the salty oak that rises to the surface.

FINISH Medium to long with increasing dry oaks. The sherry hangs about, as does the spice although the final battle is between soft lingering soft malt and a dry oakyness.

COMMENTS An all-round excellent whisky of great aplomb. The nose is nothing short of sensational and the overall balance is highly impressive with the oaky dryness always being kept in check by a lingering malty sweetness. A whisky for the connoisseur with time on his hands.

SCOTTISH LEADER

Blenders and distillers Burn Stewart date from the 1940s but since a venture capital buy-out by leading figures within the industry has specialised in producing a high number of own-label brands for supermarkets and private customers. However, one of the investors, blender Billy Walker, seems not to have overlooked the quality of their main blend, Scottish Leader (a blend which had been on the scene for many years), which although popular in pockets of Europe deserves much better attention in the United Kingdom. To keep pace with their expansion, they first bought Deanston distillery from Invergordon in 1990 and followed up three years later by rescuing the Tobermory distillery on Mull from a twilight life of being only sporadically operational.

ABOUT THE BLEND

Blender Billy Walker swears by Aberfeldy and Calo Ila and both play vital though opposing roles among the malts. The Caol Ila also adds age – up to 8 years – and Miltonduff adds to the gloss. Girvan heads the grains with North British.

NOSE A forcefully bullish nose with peat and spice making for an interesting aroma. The grains are there but incredibly soft.

TASTE Automatically mouth-filling and lush. Again the spice soars into the roof of the mouth from the start and the malt is deliciously dense and chewy. Deftly oiled to cling to the palate and malty sweet. Just a slight hint of caramel.

FINISH Long with a hint of licorice and barley sugar. The oak arrives late but puts a drying brake on the complexity of before.

COMMENTS Stupendous whisky for a brand that is meant to be fighting it out with the bottom price markers. Usually in that case the blender tends towards lack of character for safety. This, though, has personality by the barrelful and refuses to lie down and die. A whisky I tend to take to parties to guarantee a talking point and impress people. Just the odd bottle can offer a strange, juniper-type aroma. Even so, a whisky no home should be without.

FAMILY BLENDS
SCOTTISH LEADER AGED OVER 15 YEARS
A sweeter, softer aroma shows virtually no grains at all. Lots of subtle oak, though, which reveals just a hint of fine cognac. Fabulously silky and sweet on the palate with ripe greengages, cherries and delicate spices blending beautifully. The finish carries on the complexity and concludes with almonds and oak. Excellent.

SCOTTISH LEADER AGED OVER 25 YEARS
More very old cognac on the nose but now mingling with bourbon from the grain. There are also delicious tones of molten mocha.

Fabulously mouth-watering with a big arrival of high-class Speysiders and some flatter malty notes besides. A cappuccino finale as the spice and oak rumble to the enormously long finish. This is nothing short of brilliant. Because where others have failed at around this age, somehow despite all the cognac and bourbon trappings this has remained unmistakable and proudly a Scotch to the very end.

STEWART'S CREAM OF THE BARLEY

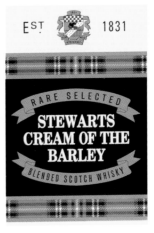

Not many blending companies that made it into the late 20th century can trace their roots back to a pub. But that was the case with Stewart & Son of Dundee before they became part of what is now Allied Domecq in 1969. Alexander Stewart had formed his reputation for whisky-dealing from 1831 onwards when he ran the Glengarry Inn in Dundee's Castle Street. It has been only in recent years that the Dundee operation was completely shut down and moved to Dumbarton, effectively ending Dundee's position as a whisky town. Curiously, before

Allied repackaged Cream of the Barley as a low-budget whisky, the brand was known as Century Hyatt Cream of the Barley. As Stewart's, though, it has shot to Number 1 best-seller in Ireland.

ABOUT THE BLEND
Despite being a value for money brand, a quite amazing fifty malts are to be found in this whisky. Somewhere.

NOSE Limited development. Although a light whisky, there is something clingingly oily and intense. The grains tend to shape what little character there is.

TASTE Sweet, fat, corn-oily with a build-up of vanilla.

FINISH Simple, soft, lightly spiced.

COMMENTS For years I really didn't like this whisky at all. Of late its rough edges have been rounded and where once this brand slaughtered the taste buds on site, now it just kind of ignores them. It has an amazing following of drinkers, especially in Ireland where it is Number 1 Scotch. But for me this is a nothing whisky, one I now neither like nor dislike. As a blend it is all terribly disappointing.

TEACHER'S

Once, Teacher's whisky was as synonymous with Glasgow as the Gorbals, the Clyde, and the rivalry between Celtic and Rangers football clubs. Today, however, the Gorbals has been redeveloped and tidied, the Clyde is all but silent and the two soccer clubs are littered with players with distinctly un-Scottish names. Teacher's, though, has run true to form as an unfaltering and sturdy keeper of Scottish tradition. It is, quite frankly, about as quintessential a Scotch as you are likely to find and that would be great news to William Teacher, the man who started it all way back in the 1830s.

It is refreshing to learn that in the conservative world of Scotch whisky the young William Teacher was a rebel. During the 1820s and 30s a tract of Scotland running from the Clyde to the Forth embraced industrialisation. With the damp climate helping the cotton industry and large deposits of coal to be mined as vital support to all others, the entire central Lowlands became a major industrial area. William first worked the cotton mills but his acute desire for social justice saw him marching against the poor conditions workers found themselves in, and on one occasion he even climbed a factory roof, amid cheers, to hoist a reformist flag. He was able to escape this grim world when, aged 23, he married into the MacDonald family that had two generations earlier seen Flora MacDonald protect Bonnie Prince Charlie.

His in-laws owned a grocery shop in Anderston, a mile or two from the centre of Glasgow, and as soon as he began work there, he turned his attention to the profitability of whisky. First he gained a licence for whisky to be consumed on part of the premises and then struck upon the idea of opening "dram shops". These institutions, unique to Teacher's, took off throughout Glasgow. People could not buy rounds in them, they were kept spotlessly clean and the only drink you could buy was Teacher's: no ale or porter or any other spirit. These shops were individually lettered and became an institution in Glasgow until they died out in the 1960s.

Throughout that time the company had remained in the hands of the Teacher family and their direct relatives, the Bergiuses, although now it is an integral part of Allied Domecq. The end of independence came in 1976 when Teacher's approached Allied Breweries in a bid to find greater financial stability. By that time Allied found themselves acquiring not just a brand but two distilleries as well. To keep pace with the success of their new blend, the Teachers built the formidable Ardmore distillery in Aberdeenshire, which came on stream in 1899, and much later bought Glendronach in 1960. But it was the Teacher's name that was most highly prized. The famous "Highland Cream" tag had been used from 1884 and the label had been virtually unchanged since then. With Whyte & Mackay

Opposite
William Teacher came up with the idea of the "dram shop", where people could go to drink whisky: no ale or porter or any other brand or spirit could be bought there. These dram shops were exclusive to Teacher's and remained an institution in the Glasgow area until the 1960s.

Above
William Teacher,
founder of the
famous blend,
was a rebel in his
time.

the Teacher's label had gone the longest without any significant alteration of design. The former has now been revamped entirely. Allied, so I have been thoroughly assured, have no such similar plans to alter its image. In many ways that just about sums up this most reassuringly solid bastion of Scotch whisky.

ABOUT THE BLEND

It is wrong to say that the more malt you tip into a blend, the better it always becomes. But the fact that there is 45 per cent malt being used in this blend obviously does no harm at all, and the style of malts is pretty impressive, too. Historically the heavily peated Aberdeenshire gem Ardmore plays a key role in this blend, and stars at the finish especially. Glendronach is also a main player and of the four grains included North British is the most impressive outsider.

NOSE Unashamedly full-bodied and rich. A delicate sweetness fails to hide a much more intense agenda. The grain is evident and keen throughout but is firmly held in check by powering peat and intense, fruity malt. A quite beguiling mixture of juicy sensual oils, apple, sweet pipe smoke and a worn, lightly polished old Chesterfield chair. Reassuringly magnificent.

TASTE Immediately opens up on the palate and swamps the taste buds with toffee-intense malt, the thin, harder grain fighting to counter the deep peat smoke. Fantastic depth and wonderful bittersweet theme throughout. Occasionally leathery, always chewy.

FINISH Long; the grain continues with some oaky, vaguely sappy age and then a tell-tale kipper finale of oil and smoke.

COMMENTS There are some people who regard themselves as whisky connoisseurs who for a social drink will taste nothing other than Teacher's. I can quite understand why. I remember first discovering the unbridled fullness of this whisky in around 1980 when former Miss World organiser Julia Morley gave me a bottle for Christmas. A love affair began that year...but not with a member of Miss World. I did actually date a Miss World contestant but my love was reserved for the whisky. Astonishingly this whisky has actually improved almost year on year. Today this phenomenal whisky remains one of the most consistent and powering blends you can treat yourself to.

TE BHEAG

This is probably the first Scotch produced with Scots in mind, and those of us born outside that land of mountain and glen can enjoy gatecrashing the party. The company, Praban na Linne Ltd, is based on the Isle of Skye, the only whisky company these days that is. Founded by Sir Peter Noble in 1976 with the further aim of helping the fragile west coast economy, the label proudly uses Gaelic: Te Bheag is a common Gaelic term for "the wee one". Even Praban na Linne means "the little whisky centre by the sound of the sleat". The blending is carried out for them by Gordon Doctor of another independent Scotch whisky company, Ian Macleod. For my money, though, the company deserves all the success it gets by having the bravery and good sense to produce a Scotch in Connoisseurs Blend that has not been chill filtered and is available as nature – and Scotsmen – originally intended.

TE BHEAG CONNOISSEURS BLEND
ABOUT THE BLEND

Blended on a similar theme to MacLeod's Isle of Skye, although with a fraction less peat. There is around 35 per cent malt content with Lagavulin and Talisker heading the cast but the Speysiders Tamdhu, Glen Rothes lighten things up with Glenfarclas adding superb top dressing. North British represents the grain.

NOSE Salty and biscuity (digestive) at first but as the whisky warms there is a much more pronounced lemony citrus freshness weighted down by the smell of drying Kentucky tobacco leaves. Extremely clean malt and a good, although easy-going, peaty background. Slightly nutty, too.

TASTE The grains, so shy on the nose, are not afraid to make their presence felt from the start. Quite a hard body with a slow malt development. Begins bracingly dry but the sweetness mounts as the complexity increases. The middle is very flitting and tangy with the citrus theme returning.

FINISH Dries as the grain sees off the malt and some powdery cocoa notes arrive. Quite a long finale with impressive, salty complexity. Some vanilla oakyness is evident.

COMMENTS An outstanding whisky for those who like to think about their dram. The complexity continues from the first nose to the dying embers of the finish and although at times it seems as though the grain has gained too much of the upper hand, the balance and poise of the whisky sees the pendulum swing back towards the malts. Light in texture, medium-bodied in weight, heavy in flavour and character. A quite exceptional blend of awesome complexity.

TE BHEAG
An altogether different animal. Sweeter on the nose and on the initial swoop across the palate and lacking those high, teasing citrus notes. The peat is nothing like so pronounced or delicate but rather acts as a blanket counter to the toffee-vanilla sweetness. The grains arrive later and are less pronounced. A fatter slightly spicier and beautifully weighted whisky of considerable charm. But for those looking for something a bit special, not a patch on the fabulous Connoisseurs Blend.

FAMILY BLENDS
MacNamara
For a whisky that means "The Son of the Sea" this is less coastal than the un-chillfiltered Te Bheag. Just a waft of peat reek on the wind hits the nose, but the citrus notes stand out on aroma and palate. A light and well balanced if uneventful blend in which the grain has by far the biggest say over the delicate malt.

VAT 69

The story behind this blend probably gives one of the earliest examples in market research the whisky industry is ever likely to

find. The Leith blender William Sanderson had been trained not just in wine and spirits, but also in the making of cordials. But he clearly saw the importance of the development of blended Scotch whisky and brought together a number of people whose palate he respected. He offered them all some 100 or so vattings he had made and together they decided the pick of the bunch was number 69: Vat 69, in fact. That was in 1882 when the use of grain whisky had become an accepted custom. However, when he started up business

some twenty years earlier his first mixture had
been taken from Glenlivet and Pitlochry
whiskies, similar to those preferred by Arthur
Bell. The brand gained some notoriety in 1914
and again in 1921 when Shackleton took it with
him on his famous Antarctic expeditions – for
medicinal purposes, of course! However, in 1937
William Sanderson became yet another cog in
the DCL machine, although for the previous two
years it had been part of the Booths Gin company.
The whisky is today available in the UK after a
period of exile as an export brand only.

Opposite
William
Sanderson saw
the importance of
the development
of blended Scotch
in 1882 when he
created Vat 69.

ABOUT THE BLEND

There are two VAT 69s. There is a the British
version which boasts 35 per cent malt or more.
And there is one for elsewhere in the world that
contains noticeably more grain. The UK blend is
easily the pick of the two and is served ebulliently
by Clynelish with two heavy-ish Speysides,
Linkwood and Dailuaine, giving a good malt
base. Malt from the little-known Teaninich
distillery aids Clynelish by giving a clean,
moderate sweetness.

NOSE Light and charming with butterfly-soft notes of clean,
unbelievably fresh Speyside malt. The grain intermingles but shows
respect to the malt and a sub-strata of delicate peat. Very evocative.

TASTE A superb mouthful of juicy grassy malt and slightly heavier smoke. The grain also fills the mouth but positively so. The result is a tastebud-quivering, mouth-watering complexity. Unbelievably fresh and even thirst quenching.

FINISH Echoes of grain, but only in a sweet-ish vanilla and drier oak. Still a very distant peatyness survives.

COMMENTS This is glorious whisky that somehow remains firmly on the light side despite having a firm smoky base. Clever, mouth-watering stuff: a fine exhibition of the blender's art.

VAT 69 (EXPORT VERSION)

(Look for 75cl bottles, a coloured royal coat-of-arms and the name of the importer on label)
One of the grainiest of the UDV blends with a warming spirit kick. There's a real fiery bite to the nose and the malt struggles to make its presence felt. To taste, enormous grains at first and rather unwieldy. But then, like blue sky appearing after the dark clouds, the blend softens and some harmonious and highly attractive malt-oily notes arrive. The malt sweetness is quite enriching and plays a good decoy to the gathering peat and chocolate. Becomes rather nutty as the grain holds firm and finally

astringent. William Sanderson would never recognise this as the prize blend that won his little contest. The flavour profile is quite striking but it never even thinks about showing complexity. If you are going to try Vat 69 for the first time, do so in Britain: this is not a patch on the home market version.

WHITE HORSE

Unquestionably one of Scotland's proudest blends, it takes its name from an ancient Edinburgh coaching inn, visited by luminaries as diverse as Dr Johnson and military aides of Bonny Prince Charlie, and which was for centuries owned by the Mackie family. By the turn of the 20th century the Mackie name was one of the most notable within the Scotch whisky industry. By then the company was in the control of the maverick distiller "Restless Peter" Mackie, renowned for an uneven temperament which would be displayed to staff and fellow whisky magnates alike. His heart and soul was in the making and blending of whisky; he was a firm advocate of using aged whiskies and unlike most of his contemporaries had learned his trade at a distillery.

Below
The maverick distiller, "Restless" Peter Mackie – "one-third genius, one-third megalomaniac, one-third eccentric."

That was at Lagavulin on Islay which had been bought in 1856 by company founder James Logan Mackie, Peter Mackie's uncle. Uncle welcomed nephew aboard the firm in 1878. Two years later J. L. Mackie set up a company called White Horse Distillers. The blend is likely to have been formulated some time in the 1880s although it was with Peter Mackie's promotion to senior partner in 1890 that the brand really started taking off. He registered the name the following year and over the following decades promoted it heavily and with almost ruthless energy. He had an answer to every problem (his motto was "Nothing is Impossible") and when buyers began turning their backs on his Hazelburn whisky because of the declining reputation of Campbeltown whisky, he wrote to blenders informing them that Hazelburn no longer made Campbeltown whisky but Kintyre whisky! Memorably, Sir Robert Bruce Lockhart in his outstanding book *Scotch* described Restless Peter as "one-third genius, one-third megalomaniac, one-third eccentric" and that would have been just about how his peers would have viewed him, especially Dewar's director A. J. Cameron who, in a private letter during takeover negotiations, wrote of Mackie: "You must be very wary when dealing with him. He plays the 'village idiot' to perfection, but is all the time picking up information". In his younger days it is likely that Mackie expressed that the all-consuming DCL

would buy them out over his dead body, which is exactly what happened. "Restless Peter" died in 1924; DCL gained control three years later. In fact, by the early 1920s Mackie had been looking to sell the company mainly because of lack of stocks but also because his son who had been groomed to take over the business had been killed in the Great War. However, Dewar's, who had considered the proposal, were looking at ditching the White Horse brand, a point that Peter could never countenance. He would, in the end, have been delighted at the deal struck with DCL and the manner in which they developed the brand. Between his death and the takeover

Above

Mackie's eccentricity is reflected in this bizarre caricature of the Scottish whisky-drinking man.

White Horse had become the first whisky to dispense with corks and use a screw cap. He would have been proud of that small last independent hurrah.

ABOUT THE BLEND

Due to its wonderful success as a single malt, Lagavulin, the blend's most traditional and famous ingredient, is now only included in seriously rationed amounts. Another White Horse malt, Glen Elgin, has no guaranteed place in the recipe at all. Instead Talisker adds much of the smoke and Glenlossie, Linkwood and Clynelish provide the sheen. The malt content can sometimes be found to be around a stunning 40 per cent while the average age of the blend is about six.

NOSE Very old-fashioned nose with a less than subtle mixture of sharp grains, clean malt and earthy peat. This is just how I first remember Scotch blended whisky to be when I was introduced to it some twenty-five years ago. What makes this particularly attractive is that when cool or when water is added these characters are compartmentalised, which is

sometimes just how I like it. But warm in the hand and you see another side to this whisky: much more honeyed, silky and integrated.

TASTE The crisp grains are given a clear sight of the taste buds before the malts catch up. This maltiness is three-tiered, with elegant, sweet Speysiders having a battle with some richer but less distinctive flat notes and then the rumble of peat.

FINISH Grain returns, bringing some vanilla and just a hint of oak. Not as complex as it once was.

COMMENTS This blend is always a sheer delight to experience and still keeping to the earthy Islay blueprint. Some vattings tend to be just a little sweeter and more honey-dominant than others, but the overall standard is exceptionally high. The finish of late, though, has been just a little lacking from time to time. But, overall, a stunning whisky that can always be found somewhere around my living room, kitchen or office.

WHITE HORSE AGED 12 YEARS

The nose displays lots of clean and sweet oloroso and impressive oak. Just as the nose suggests, this is subtly sweet on the palate with an excellent burst of rich, grassy Speyside notes. The peat lingers delightfully before a firm grain takes a grip. Pleasant honey-vanilla notes continue and vie at the death with some plummy, sherry notes. Classy stuff. For the Japanese market only and has replaced the earthier, fabulously complex and perfectly balanced White Horse 8-year-old, which was my favourite of them all but now has been tragically discontinued as a brand.

WHYTE & MACKAY

Very few whiskies in the world enjoy a lineage quite so strong or long as Whyte & Mackay. Whyte & Mackay Special began life very soon after James Whyte and Charles Mackay became partners in a Glasgow whisky merchant's and bonded warehousing business in 1882. The firm was based on the old Allan & Poynter partnership that dated back to 1844 and had been latterly run by Whyte. Although the whisky was available in limited quantities in Britain, by far its biggest markets were the English-speaking countries of Canada, USA, New Zealand and Australia. It was only after the Second World War that the company made greater strides into the home trade and they never looked back. The label had remained almost unaltered for nearly a century until a minor change in the early 1990s. But in 1998 there was a major redesign with the label moving from creamy white to blue. And it also made a point about the company's traditional double-marrying process of vatting the malts together for three months before adding it to the grains for a further three months of mingling.

ABOUT THE BLEND

A blend that goes through a double marriage. The 36 malts, aged between 4 and 8 years, are vatted together in oak butts for around four months before being added to six different grains for a further four months marrying. Because of this process there are no leading malts in the recipe.

1844   1915   1940   1950   1980   1985   1990   1998

NOSE A big, brooding, unfettered nose with quite breathtaking fruit notes. Dates and walnuts vie with plums and a squeeze of lime. The grain is soft and sexy and adds to the overall sweetness.

TASTE Fat with gentle grains to start then a tasty arrival of sweet malt. A rush of silky grains to follow through. Clever bitter-sweet balance and a delightful spice build-up.

FINISH At first remains fat and sweetish and then there are waves of vanilla and soft oak. As it dries, the grain becomes a lot more noticeable and tends to clean away the malt.

COMMENTS A really chewy blend with enormous character development. The malts tend to combine together to form a big malty middle without any particular style of malt being identifiable. Perhaps this is because of Whyte & Mackay's marrying process. This blend tends to get better as years go by. In Duty Free there is a version bottled at 105 American Proof (52.5 per cent ABV) which seems much more intensely sweet in the middle with big vanilla towards the finish.

FAMILY BLENDS
WHYTE & MACKAY 15-YEARS-OLD
A sexy, sultry nose that is top of its range for its age. Impressively honeyed and delicately oaked, there are also the mouth-watering properties of moist date and walnut cake. No less fat and rich on the palate, the taste buds are over-run with honey, a mango sweetness and melt-in-the-mouth vanilla. Brilliant grain interplay adds to the complexity. A connoisseur's whisky of distinction, much more majestic than either the mouth-watering but coarser 12-y-o or the sweeter and lusher 18-y-o Founder's Reserve.

WHYTE & MACKAY 21-YEARS-OLD
With the whisky bottled in an elegant manner which tends to show the blend in all its stunning chestnut clarity, it is no surprise that this nose is one of the most superb offered by a Scottish distiller. Subtle oloroso and peat notes mingle gloriously with a grassy maltiness that one associates with whiskies half this age. Absolutely

no sign of over-ageing on the nose, the fabulous sweet bourbon apart. Oakier and spicier on the palate than the nose suggests, this is luxurious whisky full of honey and soft sherry notes. The finish is like a whisky-rich old fruit cake with hints of dark chocolate and vanilla. Perhaps the most brilliantly balanced of all Scotland's super de luxe oldie blends. A masterpiece.

WILLIAM LAWSON

This is one of the few main blending companies to have made a successful move from England to Scotland. William Lawson had been set up in Liverpool soon after the end of the Second World War as a blending and exporting company but moved in 1967 – lock, stock and barrel – to Main Street, Coatbridge, opposite Third Division Albion Rover's now dilapidated Cliftonhill stadium. Indeed, the advertising hoardings for William Lawson situated behind the goals are about the only ones I have ever seen in this country. However, as if to underline how the company are moving up-market, in May 1998 their head office was relocated to a site overlooking Parkhead, home of newly crowned Scottish League Champions Celtic FC. To this day the company has concentrated its efforts on the export market. This has been aided by their becoming part of the Martini Rossi empire, and now part of Bacardi; until that company's dramatic purchase of Dewar in 1998, it was the

**DISTILLED, MATURED
AND BOTTLED IN SCOTLAND**

WILLIAM LAWSON'S

Finest Blended Scotch Whisky

**WILLIAM LAWSON DISTILLERS LTD.
COATBRIDGE AND MACDUFF SCOTLAND
ESTABLISHED 1849
100% SCOTCH WHISKIES**

rum company's only Scotch whisky. Oddly enough, Lawson's mirrors Dewar's pedigree dating back to the 1840s. The original William Lawson founded his firm in Dundee in 1849 although his whisky enterprise was doomed to failure. The company had been silent many years before it resurfaced in Liverpool.

WILLIAM LAWSON'S FINEST

A heavier dram on the nose with bronze where the 12-year-old offers gold. The slightly metallic graininess actually sits well with some firm malts and on the palate breaks out into a softer, much spicier dram. There is a much starker sweetness and the vaguest hints of peat-less smoke adds some counter-weight. Really good all-round whisky of the old school but with only a suspicion of Scottish Gold's mastery. Even so, this is a decent, highly enjoyable dram in its own right.

WILLIAM LAWSON SCOTTISH GOLD
12 YEAR-OLD

ABOUT THE BLEND

This is one of the most remarkably consistent Scotch blends of them all. Not a drop of Islay finds its way into the blend, which is about 45 per cent malt rich. Pride of place goes to the Speysiders, and there is a considerable top-dressing of the region's finest that shine through. So does the honey tone of Lawson's own MacDuff distillery in Banff (marketed as a single malt by the name of Glen Deveron). However, for me it is the grain which is the secret behind the blend: only maize is used (therefore from North British and Dumbarton and possibly Cambus) as opposed to wheat, which guarantees a crisper, sharper flavour. In the younger standard brand it is evident that smokier non-Islay malts are used.

NOSE Supreme honeyed sweetness, but merely dabbed on rather than pasted. The grains, despite their years, are crisp which accentuates the subtle malty, herbal, vaguely citric aroma. A hint of mint and a twist of lime complement the light vanilla oakyness. Overall, nothing short of fabulous.

TASTE The most delicate of bittersweet entrances with that honey theme remaining a golden thread all the way through. The maltiness is distinctly Speyside in character but there are slightly more earthy Highland tones too. The grain is unbelievably clean, offers the perfect spirit bite one seeks in a blend, yet is almost cathartic in quality, leaving the palate with one of the most uncluttered and complex collection of Scotch styles it is ever likely to find.

FINISH Medium length with a soft build-up of vanilla and tangerine. Some mocha notes leaves the palate almost completely satiated. This is almost too good to be true.

COMMENTS I first tasted this whisky about six years ago and was completely bowled over. It is hard to believe that any blender can continue to produce a whisky so consistently delicate for such a long time without losing quality. Blender Tom Aitken has achieved it. Although my own preference is for more full-bodied Islay-swayed drams, and this is diametrically opposed to that style, I rate it among the top ten whiskies in the world. For its style, this is as close to perfection as dammit. Sheer 70% proof brilliance.

FAMILY BLENDS
Pinwinnie Royale
A light blend also from Inver House, originally marketed in South America but now found in speciality outlets in Britain. The aroma of this 7- to 8-year-old is beautifully attractive with lovely light grainy notes carried on a honeyed breeze. That honeyed thread continues throughout the dram but becomes rather fat and chewy towards the middle. Similar in style to the Lawson's 12 but not quite so delicate. Even so, this is a stunning whisky which has improved greatly over recent years (and now signifi-

cantly sweeter) and probably reflects the far greater stocks of high-class maturing malt since Inver House's acquisition of Knockdhu seeming to have its fingerprints all over this Premier League brand.

WORLD-FAMED PRODUCT OF
THE DISTILLERS AGENCY LTD., EDINBURGH

CHAPTER SIX

DRINKING
BLENDED SCOTCH

There is only one proper way of drinking blended Scotch – or any other whisky come to that. And that is the way you prefer.

But having said that, I still cannot be convinced that there is a better way to get the most out of your blend than by drinking it neat. No ice. No water. Just a little heat applied by the warmth of your hand. Make a point of slowly nosing the glass – let those most complex aromas tickle and beguile your senses. Then raise the glass to the lips, don't sip or empty in one but pour just enough for the golden liquid to spread to every corner and crevice and then trickle slowly down the throat.

The pro-water lobby will tell you that adding a good splash of H_2O releases the aromas and softens the impact of the spirit. Which is true, but the aromas released are only at their peak for a few seconds and then the higher, most complex notes disappear. The whisky will also be slightly sweetened. And after a while it tastes just a little over-stewed.

Opposite
This character's dram is tall and neat – but the only way to drink a blended Scotch is the way you prefer.

In a way this defeats the point of a blend. By its nature it should be lighter in character than most single malts, although those using generous proportions of peaty Islays or islanders will still have enough weight to keep the taste buds humming for some time. By taking at its bottled strength you get a far clearer view of the facets that make up the brand, especially the grains and here you are likely to get a "bite" to the back of the throat that a great many blend connoisseurs, myself included, find totally irresistible.

Of course I do drink whisky and still mineral water, especially on a hot day when a few cubes of ice have been added to make a delightful long drink. Indeed, this is the way the majority of blenders prefer their dram. But don't expect to get the very best out of the whisky. Once whisky and soda was common; that has been almost entirely replaced by whisky and sparkling mineral water which I see being drunk more and more often across the world. This is far from my favourite way of drinking Scotch, but on a blazing day in California I do remember downing a glass or three.

My Uncle Dave is now well into his eighties but even from my earliest childhood recollections I can never remember him drinking anything other than whisky and dry ginger: I even recall pouring it for him when I was about seven. It remains a popular doublet but mainly among the older generation and these days it is whisky and cola that is grabbing the attention of young drinkers, especially women. If you do wish to take that road, you will get a better result using Johnnie Walker Black Label or Teachers as opposed to the corner shop's Hamish MacSporren's Old Three-Year-Old Super Cheapie, although the latter is almost certainly deserving of its death by CO_2.

The finest blends which I have gone to pains to point out in this book should be treated with the some respect afforded single malts: select a non-tumbler bulbous wine-type – preferably tulip-shaped – glass, spend some time getting to know its scent, then drink slowly. There is nothing to stop you adding water and ice – or anything else – if you wish. But only after you have become acquainted with the blend at full strength. It seems a shame not to at least give that whisky a chance to show its naked, unfettered talents when both nature and a great many people have gone to so much trouble and performed so many wonders to bring to you something of such awesome beauty.

INDEX

Acknowledgements

As is usually the case with books of this limited size, space prevents me from mentioning each and every person who has somehow made a telling contribution into the production of what is, if nothing else, a first in whisky literature.

No other book had previously been dedicated to the noble blended Scotch whisky and because of that over 100 people have been contacted by me during the course of my researches. To each and everyone, I would wish to convey my heart-felt thanks.

In particular I am endebted to that small band of people within the whisky industry, the blenders, who so willingly gave up their time, and in some cases secrets, in order for people to perhaps have a better understanding of a whisky form that has been so badly overlooked in recent years.

Those include Tom Aitken of William Lawson, now Dewar's; David Boyd (Campbell Distillers); Gordon Doctor (Ian McCleod and Co); Eddie Drummond (Inver House); Robert Hicks (Allied Domecq); Max McFarlane (Robertson and Baxter); Frank McHardy (Springbank); Robert McIlroy (UDV); Ewan MacIntosh (Gordon and Macphail); Norman Mathison (Invergordon); Jim Milne (of the Tomatin Distillery Co.); Gordon Neilson (United Distillers and Vintners); Colin Scott (Seagram); John Smith (Glenmorangie); David Stewart (Grants); Ian Urquhart (Gordon and Macphail; Billy Walker (Burn Stewart). These people have not only contributed directly to this book, but indirectly over a decade now in their patient administering of advice to me, both oral and practical. Others over the years I must thank are Stuart Nelson, Jack Goudy, Ian Grieve, Charles Craig, Jimmy Lang, Donald Mackinlay, to name but a few. Also many thanks to that least mad of scientists, Dr. Jim Swan, for popping up with that little extra bit of info when most needed.

Also I would like to thank Barry Winkleman of Prion Books to be the only publisher to have the foresight to go full steam ahead with the first ever book on blends, when every other publisher I spoke to shied away from the subject; also to Makie, my girlfriend, for being totally ignored during the months I wrote this book yet forgave me and still came back for more (and also helping out with pouring samples etc.); my secretary Di Crook for organising the delivery of the many hundreds of samples I tasted; my housekeeper Julie Musgrove for washing literally thousands of glasses and not smashing one; and finally my children, Tabitha, David and James for enduring, with Makie, my singlemindedness during the production of this book.